Science and Technology Museums

Leicester Museum Studies Series
General Editor: Dr Susan M. Pearce

Science and Technology Museums

Stella V. F. Butler

Leicester University Press
Leicester, London and New York

Distributed exclusively in the United States and Canada by ST. MARTIN'S PRESS

© Stella V. F. Butler, 1992

First published in Great Britain in 1992 by Leicester University Press
(a division of Pinter Publishers Limited)

Editorial offices
Fielding Johnson Building, University of Leicester,
Leicester, LE1 7RH, England

Trade and other enquiries
25 Floral Street, London, WC2E 9DS
and St. Martin's Press, 175 Fifth Avenue, New York, NY 10010, USA

British Library Cataloguing in Publication Data
A CIP catalogue record for this book is available from the
British Library

ISBN 0 7185 1357 6

Library of Congress Cataloging-in-Publication Data
A CIP catalog record for this book is available from the
Library of Congress

Typeset by Mayhew Typesetting, Rhayader, Powys
Printed and bound in Great Britain by Biddles Ltd of Guildford and Kings Lynn

Contents

For my father,
Jack Butler, 1924-1988

General preface to series

Museums are an international growth area. The number of museums in the world is now very large, embracing some 13,500 in Europe, of which 2,300 are in the United Kingdom; some 7,000 in North America; 2,800 in Australasia and Asia, and perhaps 2,000 in the rest of the world. The range of museum orientation is correspondingly varied, and covers all aspects of the natural and human heritage. Paralleling the growth in numbers comes a major development in the opportunities open to museums to play an important part in shaping cultural perceptions within their communities, as people everywhere become more aware of themselves and their surroundings.

Accordingly, museums are now reviewing and rethinking their role as the storehouses of knowledge and as the presenters to people of their relationship to their own environment and past, and to those of others. Traditional concepts of what a museum is, and how it should operate, are confronted by contemporary intellectual, social and political concerns which deal with questions like the validity of value judgements, bias in collecting and display, the de-mystifying of specialised knowledge, the protection of the environment, and the nature of our place in history.

These are all large and important areas, and the debate is an international one. The Leicester Museum Studies series is designed to make a significant contribution to the development of new theory and practice across the broad range of the museum operation. Individual volumes in the series will consider in depth particular museum areas, defined either by disciplinary field or by function. Many strands of opinion will be presented, but the series as a whole will present a body of discussion and ideas which should help to redress both the present poverty of theory and the absence of a reference collection of substantial published material, which curators everywhere currently see as a fundamental lack. The community, quite rightly, is now asking more of its museums. More must be given, and to achieve this, new directions and new perspectives must be generated. In this project, Leicester Museum Studies is designed to play its part.

SUSAN M. PEARCE
Department of Museum Studies
University of Leicester

List of illustrations

Preface and acknowledgements

Museums are fascinating places, allowing us glimpses of cultures and worlds from which we are usually excluded. As institutions they enjoy high status, presenting to visitors objects and ideas which carry considerable authority. In this book we look at science and technology museums around the world, exploring some of the issues which confront the museum professional in displaying these forms of knowledge to the public. I have not attempted to produce an exhaustive catalogue of science museums. Rather, I have tried to review the most important institutions, using wherever possible my own experience as a visitor, albeit a rather privileged professional visitor.

Science and technology are potent forces within modern society and their presentation deserves careful consideration. For we all depend upon the achievements of technology and the power that advanced scientific research has brought to medicine, electronics and other areas of modern life. Yet we live in a society which is notoriously ignorant of science. I suspect that the popular image of the scientist is still that of the white-coated boffin, oblivious to the cares of the 'real' world. There is continuing concern in industry and among educationalists to encourage a positive regard for science and technology, especially among young people, to ensure a continued supply of suitably qualified staff. These concerns clearly underlie much of the support given towards the development of hands-on science centres during the 1980s which is described in Chapter 5. Given these two unspoken mandates – to educate the public in areas of knowledge of critical importance to advanced industrial societies and to present images of science and technology which will be appealing to visitors – I have tried to explore how different museums approach their tasks. Chapters 1 and 6 discuss the nature of scientific knowledge and the implications which arise for the presentation of particular subjects in exhibition form. Science is essentially a system of ideas, and museums are generally about objects. We need therefore to assess how museum curators and designers have gone about their task of interpretation.

Many museums concerned with technology are of relatively recent origin and owe much to the so-called 'heritage phenomenon' of the 1980s. The development of several major open-air museums based on the history of industries dying or dead, is described in Chapter 4. The independent status of these museums, their reliance on volunteers and their vigour and success in fundraising from the private sector has influenced the development of all museums and has ensured a more visitor-oriented approach for the 1990s. Urban renewal forms the second subject of this chapter. Efforts to revitalise cities which were suffering the economic ravages of recession often involved projects to restore and reuse historic buildings. Museums were set up, often taking local trades and industries as the subjects of their displays. Both the open-air museums and museums set up as part of urban regeneration projects have tended to take a 'human interest' approach to the history of technology, focusing less on the nuts and bolts of invention and more on the use of technology within the workplace. Often technology is demonstrated to the public by museum staff who are able to tell visitors about its use in industry from their own experience. Technology has, in these ways, become a much more accessible subject within modern displays.

Like many people, my interest in museums dates from visits to the Science Museum and other great London institutions which my mother organised during the long summer holidays of childhood. My professional appreciation is of much more recent origin. In 1984, I joined the staff of the newly opened Greater Manchester Museum of Science and Industry. The museum was still very much in the making on an enormous site including two former railway warehouses, a goods shed and the original buildings of Liverpool Road Station, the world's first passenger railway station. There was tremendous scope for developing new ways to tell the story of science in Manchester and I was given every encouragement to think as broadly as possible about how and what to communicate to our visitors. I had previously taught science in secondary schools and had also recently completed my doctorate in the history of science. I was eager to blend both history and the new ideas of hands-on exhibits into the displays I was expected to develop. I owe a great debt of thanks to all my colleagues at the Museum of Science and Industry for the opportunities I enjoyed to learn my profession. Part of my brief was to develop an interactive science centre and I was much assisted in that task by the visits I made to institutions in North America when I travelled to the United States as an International Visitor in 1985. I am very grateful to the United States Information Agency for the trouble they took to ensure that I saw as many different projects as possible and for the contacts established for me in American museums.

Books of this nature are, of necessity, dependent on the goodwill of professional colleagues. I am indebted to all those who have answered my questions, sent me information and generally given me the benefit of their experience. I am especially grateful to Jim Bennett, Neil Cossons, Michael Gore, Patrick Greene, James Kahn, David Phillips, Jan Metcalfe, Alison Morrison-Low, Walter Rathjen, Peter Reed, Gordon Rintoul, Jennifer Sanders, Grant Slinn, A. V. Simcock, Stuart Smith and Terry Suthers. Professor Donald Cardwell encouraged my interest in the instruments of James Joule and provided solid advice on their interpretation. John Pickstone, who first introduced me to the history of science, has proved a continuing source of support. The final form of the book has benefited greatly from the keen editorial eye of Susan Pearce. Responsibility for any errors of fact or interpretation is entirely my own.

Thanks are due to the following for kindly granting me permission to reproduce photographs and illustrations: Catalyst, Widnes; Cité des Sciences et de l'Industrie, Paris, France; Deutsches Museum, Munich, Germany; The Exploratorium, San Francisco, USA; The Exploratory, Bristol; Ironbridge Gorge Museum, Telford; the Museum of Applied Arts and Sciences, Sydney, Australia; the Museum of Science and Industry in Manchester; the Ontario Science Centre, Toronto, Canada; Questacon, the National Science and Technology Centre, Canberra, Australia; the Science Museum, London, and Wigan Pier Heritage Centre, Wigan.

The manuscript was produced with the patient and expert secretarial assistance of Karen Stubbs and I am grateful for her help. No work of this kind can be produced without the forbearance of friends and family. I am grateful to my mother whose understanding and support is always appreciated, and to my daughter, Alice, through whose eyes I have seen museum displays afresh. Finally, I owe a great debt of thanks to my husband, Andrew Taylor, whose companionship and common sense made the whole project possible.

1. Science and technology in display

Modern museums are complicated institutions. Most combine the care, preservation and study of valuable objects with the staging of exhibitions. They educate and also entertain. The many thousands of museums worldwide vary enormously in size, organisation and in the source and extent of funding. Different museums place widely different emphasis on the various museum functions. And, of course, museums differ in the subjects of their collections. This book is concerned with the relatively small but nevertheless influential subset of museums whose major focus is science and technology. In later chapters we will look in detail at the origin of the most prominent of these museums. First of all we need to explore what we mean by science and technology so that we can consider how these subjects are portrayed by museums. In this chapter we will therefore examine the development, in Britain, of science and technology into their modern, highly institutionalised forms.

What we mean by 'science' and 'technology'

Definitions of science are not easy. According to Chamber's dictionary science is 'the ordered arrangement of ascertained knowledge, including the methods by which such knowledge is extended and the criteria by which its truth is tested . . . modern science includes such study and control of nature as is or might be useful to mankind' (Walker (ed.), 1988, p. 789). Essentially, what we think of as science is an endeavour to make sense of the external world by forming universal laws of nature, which are then constantly subject to revision. This means of making sense of the

1

world through science involves experiments, calculations, speculation and creative suggestions or theories. The process of scientific investigation is often highly skilled, involving the mastery of complex technology and, generally in the 1990s, the use of computers.

Definitions of technology are even more difficult. To see technology as simply applied science excludes the achievements of craftsmen and women who have employed none of the knowledge we call science and few of its techniques to produce a working engine or to control their environment in some way through gadgetry. Clearly, today, technology as used in industry draws heavily on science, and the training of personnel such as engineers involves the study of scientific knowledge and method, particularly experiment. However, the links between science and the technology of, say, water power in the eighteenth century is more problematic. Technology, more generally than science, concerns objects. It is about constructed objects that function to some purpose. This characteristic is useful for museums which are essentially concerned with material culture. Like science, technology was not well institutionalised in the UK until the second half of the nineteenth century. Before then, training was largely empirical, gained by working with an established practitioner. Over the twentieth century, technology has become a profession with engineers and industrial scientists spending many years learning a wide range of skills before being admitted to full membership of their profession.

Many historians of science regard the emergence of a scientific mode of thought as dating from 1540 to 1700 (Mason, 1962, pp. 127–266). They speak of the scientific revolution which involved a reliance on experiment and observation. Certainly, during this period the Aristotelian anthropomorphic cosmology gave way to a mechanical and impersonal world picture. However, although the philosophical framework of modern science is best regarded as having emerged during this period, the establishment of institutionalised science did not begin until the later decades of the nineteenth century (Cardwell, 1972).

That we put science and technology in museums suggests that both are highly valued, and form distinct expressions of culture within society and that like art, there are physical artefacts which can somehow tell this story. Indeed, creating museums of science-related artefacts suggests that science is more than just a knowledge system. If we begin to focus on science as an aspect of our culture, having a culture of its own, we can begin to build up a view of science not as the facts of an encyclopaedia but as a social system. For science involves shared beliefs, the theories upon which the knowledge system is based. Modern science uses its own language taught only to those who have been schooled in science through university or college. Science has its own system of communication through professional journals and seminars. Like any other social system, its members are organised into a social hierarchy with Nobel prizewinners at the top and craft technicians at the bottom.

Our understanding of the world has clearly changed through time. So, of course, has this social system of science. This book aims to review the ways in which museums have sought to communicate each of these three parameters: contemporary knowledge of the physical world; how ideas in science have changed through time; and the social system of science. Later in this chapter we will explore in more detail aspects of the structure of contemporary science and discuss to what extent it is possible for the science museums of the 1990s to record this current social system.

The major science and technology museum in the United Kingdom was founded in the second half of the nineteenth century. The Science Museum in London was intended to document achievement and, by so doing, to encourage further excellence. Until recently, few other institutions had taken on the task of collecting and documenting this form of culture. The Science Museum has presented the history of modern science, introducing visitors to modern concepts by displaying and describing the pathways of thought and the investigations which led researchers to their contemporary ideas. In contrast, science museums in the United States, generally younger institutions than their British counterparts, have tended to link more closely to the school system and to complement the curriculum taught in the classroom. There is much less emphasis on history and much more emphasis on the science itself. Over the last decade, partly as a response to this type of North American science museum, institutions in the UK have begun to encourage exploration through hands-on exhibitions. Like those across the Atlantic, these displays usually have no historical content and are designed to allow visitors a taste of scientific investigation, rather than to awe them with the achievements of the past. We will discuss further the development of this kind of exhibition both in UK museums and in new institutions usually referred to as science centres in later chapters. Firstly, however, let us review the state of science in the UK in the period during which the two best known British institutions, the Science Museum in London and the Royal Museum of Scotland in Edinburgh, were established.

Establishing science in the nineteenth century

Before 1850, it was extremely difficult in Britain to earn one's living through science, particularly through scientific research. This is not to suggest that Britain was in any way a scientific backwater. John Dalton, architect of modern chemistry, lived almost all his life in Manchester. Charles Darwin, arguably one of the most influential of Victorian thinkers, announced his theory of evolution by natural selection to the Royal Society of London, and lived all his life as an English country gentleman. There are endless other examples of those who achieved distinction through their research. However, science in pre-Victorian England was not an occupation regarded as a profession and, indeed, scientific research could not even guarantee anyone a living. Let us, therefore, try to build up a picture of the state of science in Britain at the beginning of the Victorian era, just before the major trade exhibition which initiated the founding of the institution which has become one of the most important science museums in the world.

Science did not feature on the curriculum of either of the two ancient universities in England, Oxford or Cambridge (Cardwell, 1972, pp. 51–9). At Cambridge the mathematics tripos was regarded as training in logic, and high honours in final examinations were much coveted. Both universities were collegiate institutions embodying the principles of tutorial higher education. Research was not regarded as a necessary or important function of any college fellow, to whom student teaching was largely devolved. In consequence, until the second half of the nineteenth century there were no scientific research laboratories at either institutions, and no research was carried out as part of university policy.

In contrast, the universities north of the Scottish border were based on a very different tradition (Morrell, 1972; Morrell, 1974). In Edinburgh the university boasted a strong tradition of scientific teaching, generally associated with its medical school. Teaching in

Scottish universities was based on the lecture system, which afforded a 'free market' in higher education as the lecturers were largely paid, not by salary, but by class fees. Students were not required to possess entrance qualifications and could attend whatever mixture of courses they chose. University teachers, the professors, enjoyed more or less total control over the content of their lectures. Because of the way they were paid, most responded to the demands of their audience, the students. Under this system, from the late seventeenth century onwards the universities of Edinburgh and, to a lesser extent, Glasgow had flourished, supplying the provincial towns of England with many medical men educated in all the most modern ideas. However, although scientific subjects such as chemistry and natural philosophy (what we would now call physics) were taught to students, lecturers were not expected to carry out original research, nor were they provided with the facilities which would enable them to do so. The openness of Scottish education and this tradition of science within the curriculum was important in providing examples which could be adopted by educational reformers of the early nineteenth century, most notably the followers of the political creed of Jeremy Bentham.

Under the terms of ancient statutes, students at Oxford and Cambridge were required to subscribe to the thirty-nine articles of the Church of England to enable them to become full members of the universities. Dissenters such as Methodists, Unitarians and Presbyterians were therefore all excluded from both institutions. As we have seen, both universities offered a very restricted education based largely on classics and mathematics. To many influential thinkers this emphasis was out of keeping with an age in which machinery and new methods of manufacture were creating conditions for unparalleled economic growth. 'Progress' was very much the concern of the Philosophical radicals, sometimes known as Benthamites. Two members of this circle, Joseph Hume and Henry Brougham, both Members of Parliament, were influential in the founding of University College, London, which opened in 1826 and formed the basis for the development of the University of London during the nineteenth century (Bellot, 1929).

University College was organised on Scottish lines. As at Edinburgh University, the College's medical school was regarded as an essential part of the enterprise and became the centre for science teaching. Courses in chemistry and botany were available to all college students, although in practice they were generally attended by medical students who needed a number of certificates of attendance at specified courses to qualify for their professional diplomas. No religious tests were required of students, and the college was open to all shades of religious persuasion. This openness and the consequent difficulty of including divinity within the curriculum aroused the anger of the Tory-Anglican establishment. They quickly organised a rival institution in London, King's College, to provide in the capital the opportunity for higher education based on the principles of the Anglican religion. Although King's College also offered medical education, its emphasis was generally less sympathetic to the rational-dissenting tradition which University College embodied and which fostered a sympathetic attitude towards the progressive sciences.

University College was the first instituti)n of higher education to be established in England since the collegiate foundations of the two ancient universities during the Middle Ages, but it was clearly not their natural successor. The London college is better regarded as the successor of the dissenting academies of the late eighteenth century.

Provincial towns such as Manchester and Birmingham, which experienced the rapid economic and population growth associated with the industrial revolution of the late eighteenth century, were centres where religious dissent flourished (Thackray, 1974). Although the community of Manchester Unitarians, for example, was not numerically large in relation to other religions, many of its members achieved considerable social influence and prestige. Dissenters and particularly Unitarians believed strongly in the value of rational thought and had high regard for education. A number of institutions, dissenting academies, offering a fairly high level of education, were set up for the sons and daughters of such families during the later part of the century.

In Manchester, an academy was set up in 1786 to succeed the academy at Warrington which had foundered as a result of financial troubles. Although the academy's life in Warrington had been brief, it had achieved considerable recognition for the standard of education it offered its pupils. Efforts to bring the academy to Manchester were made by a group of well-known dissenters associated with the Literary and Philosophical Society, set up in 1781, which met in the back rooms of the Cross Street Unitarian Chapel. Thomas Percival, a distinguished physician, had himself been educated at the

Warrington Academy. Others associated with the venture included the apothecary, Thomas Henry and the Unitarian minister, Thomas Barnes. In 1793, the Manchester Academy was able to secure the services of the distinguished teacher John Dalton, who went on to achieve fame as the architect of modern chemistry.

The dissenting academies of the eighteenth century were not the only manifestations of the interest in education, especially science, of the dissenting communities. We have already mentioned the Manchester Literary and Philosophical Society, founded in 1781. This provided a model for a number of other societies which were set up in towns throughout Britain. They provided a focus for social intercourse through science, a form of culture particularly attractive to rational-minded dissenters. The Manchester Lit. and Phil. became a kind of informal university for the town in the nineteenth century, providing both a forum where individuals could present original ideas, and a means of publishing the results of scientific investigations (Cardwell, 1972, p. 65; Kargon, 1977, pp. 5–14). For example, John Dalton first announced his atomic theory of matter to the Society in the 1800s; James Prescott Joule outlined the researches which led to the dynamical theory of heat in the Memoirs of the society during the 1840s. Researchers in this informal university had no teaching commitments and were all self-supporting. Science was a pastime, not a career.

Many of these philosophical societies set up museums for the benefit of members. The societies established in Leeds, Wakefield and many other towns throughout Yorkshire were typical (Brears, 1984). Collecting objects was not a primary motive; rather, collections were an inevitable result of efforts to develop a broad cultural base for the organisation. Scientific artefacts were often included, usually intended for practical purposes rather than for viewing alone. For example, apparatus was purchased for the benefit of members in Leeds, Scarborough, Sheffield, Wakefield and York. Members of the Sheffield Literary and Philosophical Society could experiment with electrical equipment such as electrostatic machines and leyden jars, and use the microscope or barometers. As centres for practical work, these institutions were not what we would regard as either science museums or even the equivalent of modern science centres. They were really libraries of apparatus.

The learning of science was regarded by many as morally beneficial and improving, and provided the inspiration, in part at least, for the founding of a number of institutions during the 1820s throughout Britain to provide education for artisans. George Birkbeck's lecture courses to mechanics organised in the 1800s provided a model for many of the Mechanics Institutes, as they became known (Cardwell, 1972, pp. 71–5; Kelly, 1962, pp. 112–34). Many of the middle-class fathers of the Institutes shared the Benthamite ideals of the founders of London University, and as at that institution, the natural sciences were prominent subjects within the curriculum. Although their popularity and success was often short-lived, the mechanics institutes do indicate the regard for, and interest in, science among the lower classes, and the perception of learning in these subjects as a means of bettering oneself. For the middle classes the institutes provided employment for lecturers in many scientific subjects, including chemistry, botany and natural philosophy. It should be said, however, that such employment was by no means secure, depending upon the popularity of the lectures themselves. Nor did such teaching appointments provide any support for research enterprises of any kind.

Despite this apparently piecemeal provision for the advancement of science and technology, the Great Exhibition of 1851 displayed to the world the great achievements of the British in many different fields of science and technology. The idea of national exhibitions had begun in France following the Revolution. Indeed, the idea of an international exhibition was also French in origin. It found expression in Britain through the energies of its organiser, Henry Cole, and the distinction of its patron, the Prince Consort (Cole, 1884). The Great Exhibition encompassed a wide range of subjects and included exhibitors of many nationalities. Its influence, as we shall explore more fully below was immense. Here we should note several immediate consequences of the exhibition. Although Britain's industrial supremacy was clear, the exhibition also displayed to visitors and judges of the various sections the skills of Germany, France and America. It was also clear that Britain lacked any system of organised technical or scientific education. The contrast with countries such as France and Germany was regarded as endangering the future of Britain's industry to compete effectively in world markets. In 1853, the government agreed to the setting-up of the Science and Art Department to develop a national system of technical education (Cardwell, 1972, p. 89). This was an enormously important development: government was beginning to take responsibility for education and science in order to aid industry. Under the auspices of this Department, the collection of exhibits remaining from the Great Exhibition became the kernel for the development of the South Kensington Museum which opened in 1857. This institution eventually split into two to form the Science Museum and the Victoria and Albert Museum. The Great Exhibition also prompted the setting-up of the Industrial Museum of Scotland in Edinburgh in 1855.

The Great Exhibition made clear the lack of professional opportunities for those wishing to pursue scientific research in Britain. By 1900, the situation was very different. During the intervening fifty years, university laboratories were endowed, teaching and research posts were established, and the beginnings of industrial research were organised. Perhaps the most significant developments were the setting-up of the provincial colleges which later achieved university status.

In 1847, John Owen, a Manchester merchant who had amassed a considerable fortune through the hatting trade, died leaving the bulk of his estate in trust for the setting-up in the city of a college of higher education based on the principles of the established universities (Kargon, 1977, pp. 153–7). His trustees established a college offering classical and mathematical education for the sons of the local middle classes. Owen had been clear in his will that the college was to be open to members of all religions; Owens College, as it was called when it opened in 1851, required no religious tests whatsoever. However, the college was not an instant success, and by 1857 there were very few students indeed. Its fortunes were reversed in the 1860s by a young German-trained chemist, Henry Roscoe, who through charismatic leadership and considerable energy transformed the college into his vision of a research-based professorial university such as he had experienced as a student in Germany. Owens College received its university charter in 1880, and its vigour and success stimulated the foundation of a number of similar institutions in other provincial towns. The establishment of a northern university also precipitated the reform of London University and stimulated at that institution support for the setting-up of research laboratories in a number of scientific subjects (Butler, 1981, pp. 119–201; Butler, 1986).

The transformation of British universities into institutions encompassing both teaching and research reminiscent of the type of

university established so successfully in a number of German towns
from 1815 cannot be attributed entirely to the setting-up of Owens
College. Rather, the success of the Manchester institution, where
Roscoe's chemistry laboratory achieved considerable distinction over
the 1860s and 1870s and where the physics department became a
widely-acknowledged centre of excellence, was part of a much wider
movement from the late 1860s to secure support for the endowment
of research science. Many of the endowments were actually made by
wealthy individuals or were amassed by raising subscriptions from a
number of individuals. These funds resulted in the building of
laboratories for research and teaching, and in the appointment of
additional staff within colleges and universities who were expected as
part of their duties to carry out original research.

At Oxford and Cambridge a series of reforms were imposed
following the deliberations of several Royal Commissions (Cardwell,
1977, pp. 137–53). The central university structure in both institutions was strengthened, and colleges were forced to make financial
contributions to facilities such as laboratories and teaching staff.
Several large endowments enabled the universities to set up important research laboratories. In 1870, the Cavendish Laboratory
opened and quickly became the centre for the development of some
of the most influential physicists of the late nineteenth and early
twentieth centuries, including Clerk Maxwell, J. J. Thompson and
Lord Rayleigh.

By the close of the nineteenth century it was possible to pursue
science as a career, either through one of the research laboratories
at a university or college, or in some cases through one of the
industrial laboratories set up in the later decades of the nineteenth
century.

What were the reasons behind this institutionalisation of science?
In contrast to the openness of scientific research in the mid-century
when qualifications and career had little relevance for many
publishing original research, by the beginning of the new century,
most individuals engaged in research belonged to institutions where
they received training, income and advancement through a rapidly-
developing career structure.

The driving force was the political manoeuvring of a number of
articulate and astute scientists, such as T. H. Huxley, Henry
Roscoe and Lyon Playfair, many of whom were deeply influenced
by the opportunities for scientific research on the continent,

particularly in Germany. Indeed, the German universities provided an important example for British higher education institutions. These advocates of reform were able to secure support for their proposals on several fronts. Firstly, by the 1870s it was becoming clear that Britain was struggling to maintain the economic supremacy she had enjoyed during the mid-century when the 1851 Exhibition had demonstrated the strength of her industries. Those industries, it was argued, would only be able to compete in world markets, and in particular compete against German rivals, if Britain developed a better system of higher education and endowed scientific and technical education. The mechanics institutes which had been set up with such fervour during the 1820s had in most cases declined over the middle years of the century. They did, however, in some instances provide a basis for the development of a more organised system of technical schools, initiated following a commission of inquiry in the 1880s, which received the support of local authorities. These new technical schools, and indeed the schools set up as a result of the Education Act of 1870, required educated staff. The expansion of the teaching profession also stimulated the development of the universities, providing a ready market of students and employment for graduates.

Reformers such as Playfair and Roscoe regarded exhibitions about scientific achievement as useful means of educating the public, a way of harnessing support for broader initiatives. Playfair joined the Science and Art Department on its foundation, and was involved in the establishment of both the South Kensington Museum and the Industrial Museum in Edinburgh (Reid, p. 151; Calder, 1984).

The establishment of education at a number of levels on a nation-wide scale during the last quarter of the nineteenth century required the support of government, both local and national. Although the financial support given by Parliament to colleges and universities was not great until well into the twentieth century, the acknowledgement both of the role of government in education and of the importance of an educated workforce for the state represented a major shift in political ideology. The *laissez-faire* attitude which had provided such stimulus for entrepreneurial activity in the earlier part of the century gave way to a view of government as the provider of a framework to enable industry to succeed in a much more complicated, advanced technological world.

Twentieth-century science

Since 1900, science has developed into a differentiated, highly skilled profession. Aspiring members of this community must undergo a prolonged training. Such training always involves the study of accepted knowledge, followed by examinations to prove competence. The student gains practical skills through the apprenticeship of assisting an established practitioner in research. Those aiming for the upper echelons of the profession must be prepared for the grind of producing a Ph.D. thesis, and possess the persistence required to achieve publication of a fully refereed paper. This formalised entry system ensures that scientists can develop their own language and conventions. This specialised language facilitates communications so that each concept need not be elaborated on every occasion. It also excludes those who have not received scientific training. This scientific language is an interesting problem for museums whose audience is generally the so-called scientifically illiterate. Museums in the 1990s seek to communicate. Their task becomes particularly difficult where science is concerned because they have to translate the speech of scientists into words that museum visitors will understand while also explaining a historical development or a physical phenomenon.

It is a very obvious fact that today there are many more people pursuing science, either as researchers, technicians or industrialists, than there were in 1875 or 1900. However, the growth of the scientific establishment is an important aspect of its nature and one which has had far-reaching historical consequences. The growth of science has been studied in great depth and its details need not concern us here. However, it is important for us to note the effects of this growth in the increasing specialisation of scientific disciplines. Today, the disciplinary boundaries of physics, chemistry and biology are still important, but are matched by finer distinctions between particle physics and fluid mechanics; between aromatic organic chemistry and inorganic chemistry; between molecular genetics and ecology, etc. These sub-units of science enable its practitioners to avoid information overload. Specialisation has been fuelled by the founding of journals to group research into narrower subject divisions. These journals allow scientists to make best use of their time by studying those papers of most relevance to their own research.

One of the most difficult aspects of modern science for museum curators has been the development of very large machines. This is particularly so in relation to particle physics, which since the Second World War has become dominated by huge particle accelerators. In other disciplines also, research work is often now organised around expensive, large apparatus. Research teams are now common, where the problem under investigation is shared out and time for work on the crucial piece of apparatus is allocated by the team leader. These machines often pose imponderable problems for the museum curator. Unlike the beautiful microscopes of the eighteenth and nineteenth centuries, modern equipment is not crafted to be aesthetically pleasing. It is often too large to fit into any museum store and almost always requires a reinforced floor because of its weight. Many pieces of modern equipment simply look like metal boxes, with control panels displaying information incomprehensible to the lay observer. Curators are well aware of the problem, and it is an issue to which we will return in later chapters.

The last aspect of modern science I want to underline is the growth of military research (Barnes, 1985, pp. 28–36). The Gulf War of 1991 made clear the application of scientific research in modern armaments. Chemical weapons in the form of lethal nerve gas were countered by drugs taken regularly by the opposing armed forces. The targeting of missiles was made astonishingly accurate by computer technology. These weapons have resulted from government support for military research and development, which began on a significant scale during and after the Second World War. Military science cannot, of course, be divorced from the civilian establishment. Many private companies and universities carry out research destined for defence applications. Similarly, many military research programmes have provided the foundation for important civilian technology. The most obvious example of the latter is the development of nuclear power stations following the development of the atomic bomb during the Second World War. This massive public spending on military research is hardly reflected at all in our science museums. Perhaps this is because of the secrecy of much of the work; perhaps it is because much of the research is of very little interest to the average museum visitor. I suspect that a more likely reason is the reluctance of the scientific community to acknowledge the military as such an important patron of its activities.

Modern science is a distinct part of our society. Scientific achievement is so highly valued that we regard science museums as worthy of financial support from government funds. We have seen that the establishment of the Science Museum in London and the Royal Scottish Museum in Edinburgh was part of the development of this modern institutionalised community. In the next chapter we will explore in more detail the history of these two museums, which have provided examples for institutions throughout the world.

2. Monuments to manufacture

The Science Museum in London is undoubtedly one of the great museums of the world. Visitors can gaze at the wonders of technology which fuelled the Industrial Revolution as well as find out how major discoveries in pure science have been achieved. The museum combines the presentation of contemporary science with the documentation and preservation of the science and technology of the past. In this chapter we will review the founding of this institution and how it has developed over the last 100 years to become one of the major pillars in the establishment of museums in the UK. In the second half of the chapter we will compare its history with the development of an industrial museum in Scotland and two other museums concerned with the history of science in England, the Whipple Museum in Cambridge and the Museum of the History of Science in Oxford.

The Great Exhibition of 1851

The Science Museum owes its origins to the great industrial exhibitions of the mid nineteenth century, promoted primarily by the Society for the Encouragement of Arts, Manufacture and Commerce, better known today as the Royal Society of Art (Cardwell, 1972, pp. 75–86). Its national exhibitions of 1847, 1848 and 1849 demonstrated the achievements of British industry. An international exhibition was suggested in 1848 by M. Buffet, the French Minister of Commerce, but failed to gain support from his fellow-countrymen. The Royal Society of Arts took up the idea and produced the 'Great Exhibition of the Works of Industry of all

15

Figure 2.1   Machinery Court: a view of the interior of the Great Exhibition.
(*Illustrated London News*, 20 September 1851, p. 380.)

Figure 2.2   The Great Exhibition was displayed in the magnificent Crystal
Palace erected specially in Hyde Park. (*Illustrated London News*, 20
September 1851.)

Nations' which was staged in the specially-built Crystal Palace in Hyde Park, London in 1851 (Beaver, 1970) (see Figures 2.1 and 2.2).

The Great Exhibition was administered by a Royal Commission under the active presidency of the Prince Consort. The most prominent commissioner and the individual generally credited with the success of the enterprise was Henry Cole (1808–1882) (Cole, 1884). Cole was the ultimate civil servant, devoting his life to public works and achieving the seeming impossible with impeccable administrative skill. He was also deeply interested in art and design. As a child he had lived in the same house as the painter William Peacock, who befriended the young boy. He joined the Society of Arts in 1846 and quickly became involved in organising their industrial exhibitions. He was admirably suited to take on the bulk of the administrative load involved in organising the Great Exhibition. He was given leave of absence from his post at the Record Office to serve on the executive committee of the Royal Commission. His most important colleague was the chemist and promoter of science, Lyon Playfair.

The Exhibition proved astoundingly successful. During the six months it was open between April and October 1851, 6,039,195 visitors travelled to Hyde Park to inspect and compare the industrial prowess of participating nations (Physick, 1982, p. 19). £256,808 was taken in entrance fees, and the Commissioners were able to announce a surplus of £186,436 (Reid, 1899, p. 140). The Royal Commission was given a supplementary charter to allow for the disposal of these funds, which were invested for educational purposes. The income from the monies is still used today, and the Royal Commission for the Exhibition of 1851 continues to be an active organisation.

Prince Albert wanted to use the funds generated by the Exhibition to lay the foundations for an institution which would 'serve to increase the means of Industrial Education and extend the influence of Science and Art upon Productive Industry' (Royal Commissioners, 1852, p. 11). He envisaged linking this institution to existing learned and artistic societies by bringing them together on one site in central London. To this end the commissioners purchased several plots of land to the south of Hyde Park. Some of these purchases were made in partnership with the government.

Quite apart from the funds created by the Exhibition, its success was enormously significant in several ways. Firstly, the displays embodied the Victorian ideals of progress. The presentation of evidence that progress was clearly to be achieved through technology and science could only further the case for better public recognition of the value of these two knowledge systems. Secondly, it created a fashion for exhibitions, which was as important for the development of an industrial museum as it was for the sense of national pride thereby engendered. Thirdly, through the system of medals awarded by judges for various categories, the Exhibition made clear that Britain's industrial supremacy was under serious threat from her fast-industrialising European neighbours. Those pressing for a better education system were quick to point out that retaining that supremacy would be difficult for a country lacking any organised system of technical or scientific education. Lyon Playfair stressed the comparison with Germany, whose system of state-funded technical schools and science-based universities provided highly skilled person-nel for Germany's increasingly sophisticated and research-dependent industries (Reid, 1899, pp. 149–50). His observations had to be taken seriously. After qualifying in medicine, he had travelled to Germany to study for a Ph.D. under Justus Liebig, the great German chemist. Playfair was well aware of the lack of opportunity in Britain. He himself had struggled to find a suitable post which would allow him to develop a scientific career and provide him with a livelihood.

The South Kensington Museum

In 1852, with the Great Exhibition behind him, Henry Cole took over as General Superintendent of the School of Design, which had been formed as a result of a government inquiry into the state of industrial design in 1836. By 1852, the school was in serious decline. Following the establishment of local schools in the large manufactur-ing cities of England, the School of Design in London had become, during the 1840s, largely a teacher training institution. When Cole took over, the school was housed in stiflingly cramped conditions at Somerset House. Cole immediately appealed to his friend the Prince Consort for help, and with his support the school was moved to Marlborough House. From its beginning the School of Art had established a collection of artefacts to be used to inspire its students to further ideas. The museum and the central school, together with the schools of design in the provinces, formed the basis for the government Department of Practical Art. Initially it came under the aegis of the Board of Trade. In 1856, the Department was renamed the Department of Science and Art and became responsible directly to the Privy Council.

From its formation, Cole acted as Secretary to the Department of Science and Art. The remit was to develop a system of technical education throughout the country relevant to the manufacturing industries. Cole was assisted by Lyon Playfair, with whom he had worked on the Great Exhibition. Playfair was by then a chemist of considerable standing, a Professor at the School of Mines who had been appointed Fellow of the Royal Society – one of the highest accolades awarded to scientists in the UK – in 1848. Playfair remained joint secretary with responsibility for science until his appointment to the Chair of Chemistry at Edinburgh University in 1858.

In 1856, the School of Design, which was eventually to become the Royal College of Art, moved to accommodation on land purchased by the Exhibition Commissioners. The object collections were displayed in iron structures which became known as the 'Brompton Boilers' (Physick, 1982, pp. 23–6). The collections gained some autonomy from the school at this stage, and the Boilers were named the South Kensington Museum. The teaching of the school was carried out in three renovated houses, and some wooden huts which were linked to the Boilers by a temporary building. In these rather hideous exhibition halls the foundations of two of Britain's best loved museums were laid – the Victoria and Albert Museum and the Science Museum.

Not surprisingly, most of the objects in the collections from the School of Design were examples of decorative arts. However, during the 1850s the school began to accumulate artefacts relating to both science and technology. Objects were purchased from the 1851 Exhibition and examples of machinery were amassed. In 1864 the collections began to be moved across to the west side of Exhibition Road into the Southern Galleries. A ship model collection was inaugurated in that year on the request of the Lords Committee of Council on Education. In 1864 the museum also acquired the Buckland fish collection from an Inspector of Salmon Fisheries.

As we have seen in Chapter 1, the state of science and particularly of scientific and technical education came under official scrutiny during the 1860s and 1870s. In 1874 the Report of the Royal Commission on Scientific Instruction was published. The Commission, under the chairmanship of the Duke of Devonshire, had been initiated by the government after considerable pressure from organisations and individuals anxious to see government action in the promotion of science and technology. Its members included some of the leading figures in science: T. H. Huxley, the great physicist G. G. Stokes, Sir John Lubbock, the physiologist William Sharpey, Lord Lansdowne, and Herbert Samuelson. Norman Lockyer was secretary (Cardwell, 1972, pp. 119–26). The Commission took evidence about the state of science teaching in the universities: Oxford and Cambridge, London and Manchester. It became clear that few students were coming forward to study science, except at Owens College, Manchester where a vigorous School of Chemistry had been established by the German-trained chemist, Henry Roscoe. Lack of professional opportunities deterred young people from pursuing a career in science. The Commission also examined the state of secondary education and found science teaching there seriously deficient, and they took evidence from those advocating radical reforms which would create careers in science through the endowment of state-funded laboratories and research institutes.

The series of reports suggested far-reaching reforms. Generally they supported those who had long been pushing for the government to provide the financial means to create a comprehensive system of scientific and technical education, together with funds for further research. They also suggested that a 'Collection of Physical and Mechanical Instruments' be assembled and merged with the collections of the Patent Museum and the Scientific Department of the South Kensington Museum to form a single museum under one Minister of State. The idea was to provide a nucleus of objects which could inspire good practice, and which could also compensate for the lack of apparatus available to many institutions by means of a system of loans (Royal Commission, 1874, p. 23). The 1851 Commissioners offered to provide a building for this proposed museum. Their offer, repeated several times, was eventually formally refused.

However, many influential figures in the scientific community continued to press for the formation of a national science museum.

In 1875, the Lords Committee of Council on Education approved a proposal to assemble and exhibit at South Kensington a Special Loan Collection of Scientific Apparatus. Everyone who was anyone in science became involved. Although the exhibition was international in scope, objects were not arranged (as was usual by then in international exhibitions) by country, but by classification of exhibit (Science Museum, 1876) (see Figure 2.3).

The exhibition was opened in 1876 by Queen Victoria. Despite its success and the pressure again exerted on the government for the setting up of a science museum, nothing happened. Nevertheless, the effort which went into organising the Special Loan Collection did not go completely unrewarded. Many of the objects brought together for the exhibition were subsequently donated to the South Kensington Museum and provided valuable material for the science collections. In 1883, the Patent Museum was acquired by the Department of Science and Art and much of the material absorbed into the science collections.

Although no moves were made to provide permanent accommodation, the growing distinction between the two sections of the South Kensington Museum were recognised in 1885 when the Department decided to designate the science collections the Science Museum. By 1890, the Art Museum had expanded considerably since the early days of 1857, when the Brompton Boilers opened their doors (see Figure 2.4). The Boilers had been removed in part to Bethnal Green where they provided accommodation for the Animal Products and Food collections. Permanent buildings had been erected between 1857 and 1861 (Physick, 1982, pp. 33–56, 143–6). New buildings to house the science schools, set up as part of the Science and Art Department, were added in 1872. Because they faced Exhibition Road, great care was taken to provide an appropriate façade. Their elaborate exterior did ample justice to Cole's vision of architectural excellence, and this building now forms the Henry Cole wing of the Victoria and Albert Museum. Further buildings created warren-like accommodation for the museum, the schools of art and science and the Department of Science and Art itself.

The Special Loan Collection had been displayed in the building to the west of Exhibition Road which had been used to house the refreshment area for the International Exhibition of 1862 (Science Museum, 1876). The science collections continued to occupy this space as the site was developed for the new Imperial College,

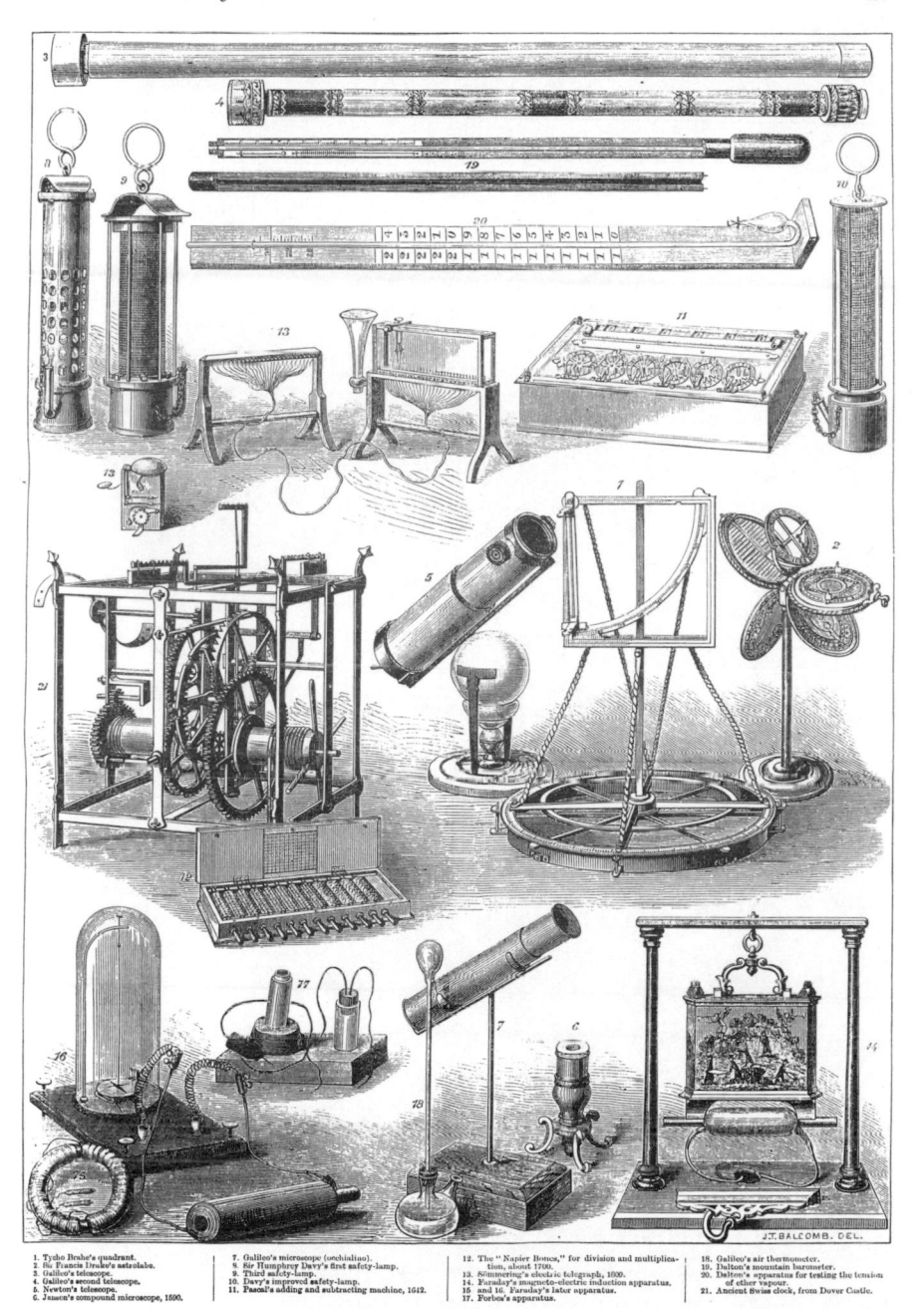

1. Tycho Brahe's quadrant.
2. Sir Francis Drake's astrolabe.
3. Galileo's telescope.
4. Galileo's second telescope.
5. Newton's telescope.
6. Jansen's compound microscope, 1590.

7. Galileo's microscope (occhialino).
8. Sir Humphrey Davy's first safety-lamp.
9. Third safety-lamp.
10. Davy's improved safety-lamp.
11. Pascal's adding and subtracting machine, 1642.

12. The "Napier Bones," for division and multiplication, about 1700.
13. Sömmering's electric telegraph, 1809.
14. Faraday's magneto-electric induction apparatus.
15. and 16. Faraday's later apparatus.
17. Forbes's apparatus.

18. Galileo's air thermometer.
19. Dalton's mountain barometer.
20. Dalton's apparatus for testing the tension of ether vapour.
21. Ancient Swiss clock, from Dover Castle.

Figure 2.3 Examples of instruments displayed in the 1876 Special Loan Collection at the Science Museum. (*Illustrated London News*, 16 September 1876, p. 269.)

Figure 2.4 The remains of the Brompton Boilers in the early years of this century. (Science Museum, London.)

formed in 1908, through an amalgamation of the Royal College of Science, the Royal School of Mines and the City and Guilds Institute Central Technical College.

Henry Cole had campaigned vigorously throughout his career for a building to do justice to his idea of a museum in the grand style. He retired in 1873 and his successors continued to press the government of the continuing need for more display space. Their cries went unheeded until 1890, when the government gave way to powerful lobbying and announced a competition for a design for a building which would utilise the area remaining on the site occupied by the Department and provide a public façade along Cromwell Road and Exhibition Road (Physick, 1982, pp. 183–200). Eight architects competed, and Aston Webb's design won. However, as Webb proceeded to prepare more detailed drawings, numerous alterations were suggested by the Office of Works and others. During the wranglings, the Director of the museum retired and he was replaced in 1893 by two equal Directors, one overseeing the Art Museum, one in charge of the Science Museum. This was an important break underlining the increasing distinction between the two sets of collections. Shortly afterwards it seemed likely that the Science and Art Department, responsible for the museum, was likely to be merged with the Education Department which had grown in influence and extent since the passing of W. E. Foster's Education Act of 1870. It seemed probable that the museums would be taken over by a body set up to oversee the burgeoning state education system.

As a result of all the political manoeuvring both within the museum and within the Department of Science and Art, a select committee was set up to look into the Department's museums at South Kensington. The committee's deliberations revealed the strength of the lobby among leading scientists of the day for new buildings for a science museum to be established alongside the Royal College of Science on the west side of Exhibition Road. Individuals such as Henry Roscoe, by then a Member of Parliament but formerly Professor of Chemistry at Owens College in Manchester, pressed the government to take steps to establish an institution which would both instruct the public in science and inspire through past achievements. Roscoe had a powerful voice, having been responsible for introducing German techniques for instruction and training in science into Britain in the 1860s and 1870s.

/ever, there was little government support for any such schemes.
: government continued to vacillate over the initiation of any
building project at South Kensington, although steps were taken to
lessen the fire risk on site by taking down particularly vulnerable
buildings. In 1899, the Science and Art Department was finally
disbanded, and responsibility for technical education as well as the
South Kensington museums was transferred to the newly-established
Board of Education. With the prospect of dissolution clearly in sight,
the Department of Science and Art continued its discussions of the
building plans for South Kensington, this time with a view to
accommodating both the art and science collections in Webb's new
building. The science lobby were as vehemently in opposition to this
plan as were the art lobbyists. Both wanted the Science Museum
housed in separate buildings to the west of Exhibition Road
(Physick, 1982, p. 207).

In the end it was decided to proceed with the original scheme put
forward in the 1890 competition by Webb, whose designs, despite
the discussions of almost eight years, emerged relatively unscathed.
The building project began in 1899 when Her Majesty graciously
consented to re-naming the museum 'The Victoria and Albert
Museum'. Building work was painfully slow, and the new buildings
were not officially opened until 1909 (Physick, 1982, pp. 213–49).

The new buildings provided opportunities for a review of the
organisation of the collections as a whole. Although the science
collections had now been recognised as a separate museum for
nearly twenty years, they were still regarded as part of this newly
fashioned 'Victoria and Albert Museum'. Under the guidance of
Robert Morant, an influential Secretary to the Board of Education,
a committee was set up to consider the organisation of gallery space
for the art collections within the new buildings, and the overall
purpose of the museum. Morant decided that it must be made clear
that the term 'Victoria and Albert Museum' applied to the art
collections only (Physick, 1982, p. 246).

An autonomus science museum

Although the opening of the new museum buildings on Exhibition
Road afforded the Science Museum true autonomy, the lack of
accommodation for displaying the now considerable amount of

material and for developing further exhibitions and activities gave little value to this new independence. However, with the Victoria and Albert Museum now in purpose-built, albeit considerably flawed accommodation, civil servants began to consider the new buildings required by a science museum. A Departmental Committee was set up in 1910 to consider, in the same way that the V. and A. was discussed, what purposes a science museum should serve and how best those purposes might be fulfilled (Report, 1911, 1912–13). The committee was chaired by Sir Hugh Bell, an industrialist, and included a number of leading academics, including the President of the Royal Society, Sir Archibald Geikie, together with a naval engineer and a shipbuilder (Follett, 1978, pp. 19–33).

The report was enormously influential and provided a long-term development plan for the museum. The committee proposed that the museum's collections should both illustrate the various branches of science and demonstrate their industrial applications. Objects should be available to scholars for study. Displays should be aimed at the general visitor possessing no specialist knowledge of science.

By 1910, the collections and the displays were organised into three divisions: Naval and Marine Engineering, Machinery and Inventions, and Scientific Apparatus. The displays were not the 'storyline' exhibitions of modern museums; rather, exhibits were described on fairly detailed labels which told the visitor how the object fitted into the history of that particular branch of science, how such objects were used and how they were made. There was also a significant number of working models, constructed in the museum's own workshops. Many were operated by compressed air or by handles on the outsides of the cases. Some of the machines in the Machinery and Inventions section were actually operated in order to demonstrate the exhibit in motion. The Bell committee endorsed these exhibition principles and emphasised the value of catalogues.

In the early days of the museum, a school loans service had operated. One value of the collections in the 1870s had been seen as that of plugging the gaps in the provision of apparatus in schools and colleges. The committee felt that this service was not worth reviving, but they did emphasise the value of the museum as an educational resource, and made various recommendations as to how the collections might be made accessible for teachers.

The committee estimated that approximately three times the current space was needed to implement their recommendations.

They suggested that 265,000 sq. ft. of exhibition space be provided in new buildings, and that the building work should be staged in three phases. The eastern block they clearly expected to be initiated immediately after the acceptance of their report; the central block would follow soon after, so that the first two phases could be completed within ten years or so; the third phase could follow as more space was required. In reality, although preparatory work on the site was begun in 1913, the First World War delayed any substantial building work and the first phase was not completed until 1928. The second phase providing the centre block was not even begun until well after the Second World War and completed only in 1962.

The final section of the Bell Report was published in 1912 (Report). The previous year, F. G. Ogilvie had succeeded W. I. Last as Director of the museum. Ogilvie and his successor, Henry Lyons, were responsible for implementing the Bell Report, and in so doing establishing the modern form of the Science Museum. Ogilvie had been a distinguished academic, the first Principal of Heriot-Watt College, a professor of Applied Physics, and from 1900–1903 he was Director of the Edinburgh Museum of Science and Art. In 1903 he left Scotland to become a civil servant at the Board of Education. In 1910 he became Secretary for the Science Museum, Geological Museum and Geological Survey, and acted as Secretary to the Bell Committee. When he became Director of the Science Museum he retained his other duties within the Board of Education. Because of this he secured the services of an assistant, and despite the relatively lowly salary of the post he persuaded Henry Lyons, who had recently left an unsatisfying lecturing post at Glasgow University, to join his staff. Lyons came to the Science Museum with an exceptional record of achievement. While serving with the Royal Engineers in Egypt during the 1890s he had established himself as an authority on that country's geology and archeology. In 1901 he became head of the Egyptian government's Survey Department. He published prodigiously and was elected a Fellow of the Royal Society in 1906. He left Egypt in 1909 to take up a lectureship in geography, but was never happy and resigned at the end of 1911. He came to the Science Museum with a considerable reputation as a scientist and an administrator, but with no experience of organising collections or setting up exhibitions. Initially Lyons was appointed to a new post as assistant to the Director and Secretary to the Advisory Council, a body recommended by the Bell Committee but not yet established. On the outbreak of war in August 1914 Lyons was recalled for military duty and he remained in the army until the war ended. When he returned to the museum in 1919 he had been promoted to Keeper. The following year he was appointed Director (Follett, 1978, pp. 35–9). As Follett has observed, the most obvious event of Lyons' directorship was the opening of the new building in 1928 (Follett, 1978, pp. 84–7). At last the museum had an appropriate frontage on Exhibition Road and display space to do justice to some of its spectacular pieces of machinery.

Ogilvie, on the publication of the Bell Report, had immediately set about improving the collections according to the committee's recommendations. Lyons continued that work, enlisting the help of established scientists through the Advisory Council establishment in 1913, which comprised distinguished engineers and academics. He issued guidelines concerning the presentation of the collections, essentially continuing the tradition established in the last quarter of the nineteenth century of serried ranks of objects with detailed labels explaining their significance. Importantly, Lyons recognised that the most important visitor was the non-specialist who probably had very little knowledge of science or engineering. The workshop continued to be important in providing working models of certain exhibits and in providing mechanisms to make a few exhibits move. Lyons codified the art of label-writing, establishing guidelines for curators about the style of each entry. He also changed the form of publications produced by the museum. In 1910, the visitor had been able to buy catalogues of exhibits which essentially reprinted the exhibit labels. This form of publication was expensive, partly because so few sold. Lyons decided to make the catalogue more readable and he introduced two sections, one a general introduction to the particular subject, and the other an illustrated catalogue of the exhibits.

Perhaps the most innovative of Lyons' projects was the Children's Gallery, opened in 1931 (Museums Association, 1931; Hartley, 1938) (see Figures 2.5 and 2.6). It was an instant success, attracting a large number of new visitors to the museum. The Children's Gallery served two main purposes. It explained in simple visual terms suitable for the very young – often dioramas – the context of many of the technical developments (for example, transport) seen elsewhere in the museum. This was the first time that the museum had tried to explain not just the technical background to its

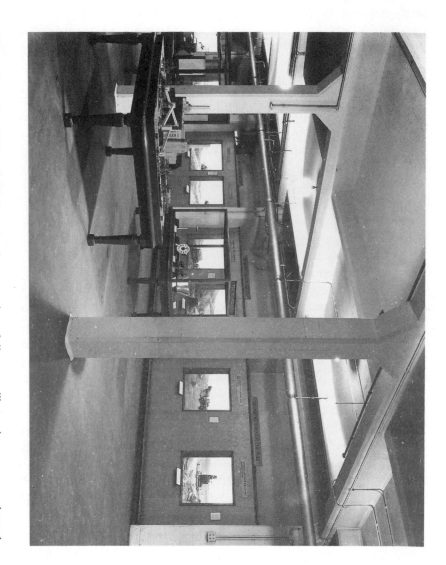

Figure 2.5 The Children's Gallery showing a number of dioramas illustrating transport through the ages. (Science Museum, London.)

Figure 2.6 Young visitors investigating time measurement in the Children's Gallery in the 1930s. (Science Museum, London.)

collections, but some of the human implications of science and engineering. The other purpose was to allow, in modern parlance, some hands-on exhibits so that children could better understand some of the principles behind the technical developments demonstrated elsewhere in the museum. This aspect of the gallery was to provide inspiration to individuals later in the century trying to build new kinds of science museum based on interactive exhibits. The Children's Gallery was also equipped with a small cinema which showed films for children at regular intervals throughout the day.

Lyons was keen to encourage temporary displays. Many under his directorship were mounted by various research organisations. He was anxious to foster closer relationships with industry, although the difficult economic times of the late 1920s and early 1930s did not make such partnerships easy. However, in 1933 the plastics industry organised a successful exhibition foreshadowing the partnerships which were to become so important to the development of the museum after the Second World War.

In 1910, approximately 400,000 visitors came to see the exhibits set out in the temporary, cramped quarters of the southern and western galleries. By 1935, double that number were visiting the new building on Exhibition Road (Greenaway, 1951, pp. 13–14). The museum had certainly proved its popular appeal. Staff looked forward to the promised centre block which would broaden the scope of displays still further, but like the east block, this was delayed by a world war. During the Second World War, the collections (with the exception of the library) were evacuated for safe-keeping and the museum buildings taken over and used for military training.

Post-war developments

Reinstalling the exhibits after the war was a long job. The impetus for more accommodation was provided by the centennial exhibition planned for 1951. Building began in 1949, and a partially completed centre block was ready for the Festival Exhibition (Greenaway, 1951). Subsequent difficulties and delays meant that the block was not fully completed until 1961 (Day, 1987). By the 1960s, the character of the museum was beginning to change in several significant ways. Firstly, exhibitions were becoming less the responsibility of individual curators and more the product of team efforts involving designers. As exhibitions became increasingly technically complex, involving an ever-broadening range of display techniques, including audio-visual presentations, films, audio handsets and theatrical 'sets', designers began to assume a prominent role in the process of putting together exhibitions. A Museum Services section of the Science Museum was set up in 1963 which included an exhibition design group. Designers began to see themselves as interpreters, arguing that where specialist subjects like science were concerned it was essential to involve professionals whose primary skill was communication. As exhibitions became more complex, so they became more expensive to stage. An exhibition under the Lyons' principle involved the cost of cases, simple typed labels and perhaps the cost of a model or device to bring objects into motion (see Figure 2.7). Today, with the costs of specialist structures on which to mount extensive, usually coloured graphics with photographic and other

Figure 2.7 The East Hall in the 1930s displaying stationary steam engines. Note the detailed labelling. (Science Museum, London.)

illustrative material, lighting, computers and television monitors, the amount of money to stage just one exhibition is usually of the order of several hundred thousand pounds (see Figure 2.8). Increasingly, the Science Museum has looked to industrial sponsorship to cover such costs.

A second important change that has taken place since the 1960s has been that the exhibitions themselves have become less to do with objects and more to do with subjects or themes. That is not to say that the objects are not still vitally important components of each exhibition, but rather that the objects have become illustrative of a story or a point being made through the exhibition. For example the Wellcome galleries, intended for a non-specialist audience, present objects from the vast and eclectic collections of the pharmaceutical magnate Henry Wellcome in a series of period sets. We will discuss

Figure 2.8   The East Hall in the 1990s: new audio-visual display techniques and modern customer care have now joined the steam engines. (Science Museum, London.)

below the implications for museums and their collections of such displays.

A third modern development has been that the museum has become much more a museum of science and people – the people who have made the discoveries, the people who are involved in the manufacturing industry, the people whose lives are affected by the science and technology on display. In 1968 the museum published a guide, *In the Science Museum*, which through readable text and stylised black and white and colour sketches provided a background social history to the museum's exhibitions (van Riemsdijk and Sharp, 1968). Like the Children's Gallery before it, the guide tried to bring to visitors the human dimension of the exhibits which might not always be apparent to the general visitor. Today, it would be unthinkable to develop a design brief for an exhibition which did not include people.

In recent decades there have been further changes. There was the introduction during the 1980s of 'hands-on' exhibits. The Science Museum has a long tradition of working exhibits, but this tradition was taken further in the development of 'Launch Pad' (discussed below). There was also the diversification away from London which began in the 1970s. The Director, Margaret Weston, took much pride in the development of the National Railway Museum at York which opened in 1976, and in 1983 the National Museum of Photography, Film and Television opened in Bradford. Both have proved huge successes, continuing the Science Museum's tradition of well-researched exhibitions with popular appeal.

Another fundamental change of recent years has been the introduction of admission charges. The principle of free admission to museums is dearly cherished by many both in and out of the museum profession. The decision to charge followed changes to the administrative structure of the museum. Following the recommendations of the Rayner Scrutiny into the management of the Victoria and Albert Museum and the Science Museum, the government set up a trust to take ultimate responsibility for the museum (Burrett, 1982). Funds from central government are made available to this trust to run the museum, but control is now at arm's length from civil servants and politicians. Under the guidance of Neil Cossons, Director from 1986, the Trust took the decision to make an entrance charge. Cossons had previously introduced charging at the National Maritime Museum and was firmly committed to the idea that it

Figure 2.9   Food for Thought: a visitor inspects a set of a 1920s shop. (Science
Museum, London.)

made for a better museum. The Victoria and Albert Museum had
already introduced charges; theirs were voluntary, and had caused
uproar among staff and members of the public, but the protests at
the Science Museum were quieter. The implications, however, are
long-term and far-reaching and indicate a wide evaluation of the
role and purposes of the museum. We will discuss these issues
further in the final chapter when we review the contemporary state
of science and technology museums and their future directions.

The range of exhibitions on display in the Science Museum in the
1990s is wide. As with any very large museum, exhibitions vary in
their presentation and style, not least as some still date from the re-
display of collections following the Second World War evacuation.
Older parts of the museum cover highly academic subjects such as
'Optics' and 'Heat and Temperature', reflecting school and college
curricula. The more modern galleries such as 'Plastics' use broader
themes which incorporate social and economic issues. Some parts of
the museum, such as the gallery presenting the biochemistry of the
living body, deal with highly technical information in a format

which non-specialist and younger visitors must find fairly inaccessible. Other sections such as Launch Pad, the museum's hands-on science centre, and the most recent interactive display, the Flight Experience, are designed to be accessible to as broad an audience as possible. Galleries developed over the last decade, such as 'The Exploration of Space' and 'Food for Thought' (see Figure 2.9), present their messages in dramatic sets, incorporating computer technology and other interactive media as well as original objects (Sudjic, 1990). The fourth and fifth floors are entirely devoted to medical themes, constituting almost a museum within a museum; the displays use the material of the Wellcome collections and are important in bringing medicine under the aegis of 'science' (see Figures 2.10, 2.11).

The Science Museum came into being in the late nineteenth century as part of the campaign to establish a scientific and technical education system in Britain. The museum was a means of demonstrating past achievements and gaining support for future developments. The Bell committee, the body which had most influence on the early development of the institution, was dominated by men who were recognised as successful scientists and engineers and who wanted to press the government to provide more resources for science and technology. Successive directors of the museum were individuals whose science or engineering credentials were impeccable and who had been involved in education. The role of the museum as public educator has always been of great importance.

The museum presents very positive views of both science and its applications; it has been created as a public showcase for science. Some years ago, attempts to present a critical appraisal of the nuclear industry met with very severe disapproval. There is little or no discussion of the process of science or how the scientific establishment in its modern form works. The museum provides what its early supporters hoped: a treasure trove of wonderful gadgetry from the past and a powerful means of promoting what we think of today as the public understanding of science.

A national museum for Scotland

The popularity and the financial success of the 1851 Great Exhibition affected the development of institutions both within and outside

Figure 2.10   The Science Museum, London. (Science Museum, London.)

London. As a Scot, Lyon Playfair wanted to see in his home town of Edinburgh a museum comparable to that being established in London. He himself negotiated with the university and with the town council, and it was agreed that the Department of Science and Art would set up an industrial museum intended to stimulate manufacturing industries through education (Reid, 1899, p. 151). The museum's first Director was George Wilson, a long-standing friend of Playfair. He began collecting widely, using Playfair's interpretation of the 'industrial' concept to mean the mineral resources of Scotland as well as objects demonstrating the manufacturing process itself (Anderson, 1989, pp. 9–10). He was also an active teacher, and used the collections to illustrate his lectures.

In 1855, the Department of Science and Art acquired the natural history collections of Edinburgh University (Anderson, 1989, pp.

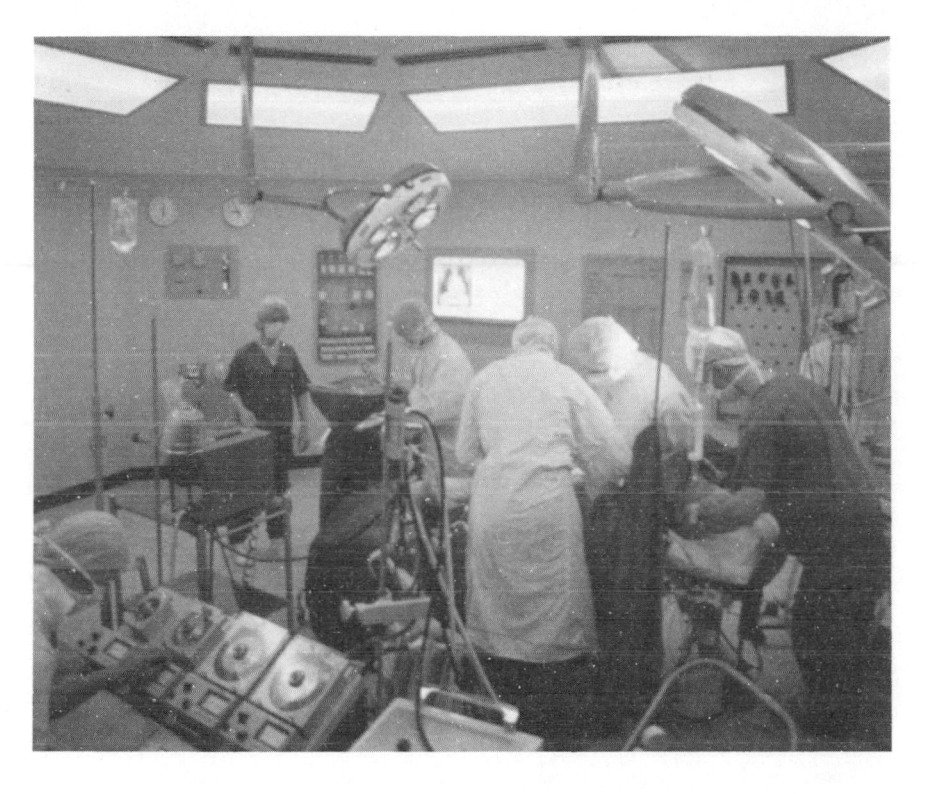

Figure 2.11 The Wellcome Galleries include several reconstructions of medical scenes. Here a modern operation is depicted using up-to-date equipment. (Science Museum, London.)

10–13). The motive behind the transfer was accommodation: the Department of Science and Art had to find a building for the new industrial museum, and that building could also provide proper display space for the natural history collections. Initially at least, the professor of Natural History at the university retained charge of the collections. In 1861 building work started on a site in Chambers Street adjacent to the university, and in 1866 the first phase opened. A bridge connected the museum to the university so that students could have convenient access to the collections. The two museums were renamed the Edinburgh Museum of Science and Art; in 1905, the museum changed its name again to the Royal Scottish Museum.

In the late nineteenth century, 'art' was taken to mean the 'arts of manufacture' – the meaning used in the titles of several international and national exhibitions. However, during the twentieth century, collecting at the Royal Scottish (now the National Museums of Scotland) became more heavily biased towards the decorative arts. Although the museum retains a strong technology collection with ship models, stationary engines displayed in a 'Hall of Power', and other objects of technical interest, the museum has become a more general institution than its cousin in South Kensington. Since the 1960s, collections of scientific instruments have been put together and valuable examples of the work of Scottish instrument-makers amassed; the museum has also been active more recently in collecting early computers and examples of some of the large machines associated with modern science.

Perhaps because of the multiplicity of its roots and the inclusion within its scope of natural history almost from the beginning, it is hard to see the Chambers Street museum as a specialist science or industrial museum. It serves the functions for Edinburgh of the three main museums in South Kensington. Nevertheless, perhaps the most important point to note is the fact that its origins stem from the success of the Great Exhibition in displaying science and technology as progressive forces within British society. Like the London Science Museum, its promoters belonged to a small but energetic group of individuals determined to create careers in science and to develop educational opportunities. George Wilson was a busy lecturer and used the museum's collections in his teaching. Playfair intended Edinburgh's museum to become a northern version of the South Kensington museums, demonstrating all that was modern and successful in science and technology and providing a platform for reforms in the system of scientific and technical education.

Museums of the history of science

The museums set up by the Science and Art Department in the mid-nineteenth century were intended to communicate to visitors information about science. They were essentially educational institutions. In contrast, a different type of museum intended primarily to commemorate rather than communicate science has come into being during the twentieth century at Britain's two most prestigious universities, Oxford and Cambridge.

By the end of the nineteenth century, the Old Ashmolean

Museum building had become neglected. A campaign to restore the fabric of the building and establish within it a collection documenting the excellence of Oxford science gathered momentum during the early years of the century, led by R. T. Gunter who was eventually to become the museum's founding curator (Gunther, 1985).

In 1924, the Lewis Evans Collection of scientific instruments was installed on the top floor of the building. Evans was a life-long collector who had amassed a large number of instruments from sale rooms. In 1935 the collection was formally constituted as a university department, the Museum of the History of Science. Gunter, the museum's first curator, was able to complement Evans' collection with material trawled from the university's many laboratories. The collections have been developed since by judicial collecting both from within the university and by purchases through the antique market.

The result is a museum providing rich primary material for the historian of science. For example, the visitor can see on display the X-ray spectrometry apparatus used by H. G. J. Moseley by means of which he demonstrated the periodicity of the elements, establishing a series of values for each element which later became known as atomic numbers. Visitors can study examples of early chemical apparatus, some used in the very basement in which it is displayed, and the craft of the scientific instrument-maker of the eighteenth and nineteenth century is also displayed to powerful effect. The instruments are examples of precision technology, often crafted by hand by the most skilful makers of the day. Today they are objects of rare beauty, often made of brass, providing us with a glimpse of the past when science was an individualistic pursuit of the well-to-do.

In Cambridge, moves to set up a museum to pay due respect to the scientific heritage of the university began in the 1930s. In 1936 the Cambridge Philosophical Society organised an exhibition of historic apparatus collected together from the various university colleges (Cambridge Philosophical Society, 1936). The following year a weekly series of lectures began on the history of science by distinguished figures such as J. D. Bernal and Sir Arthur Eddington. These were evidently popular and successful as they appear to have continued uninterrupted except for a short period during the Second World War.

In 1944, the Vice-Chancellor was able to announce the gift to the university of the collection of scientific instruments and books of Robert S. Whipple (Cambridge University, 1944). Whipple had a lifelong interest in instruments, having joined the Cambridge Scientific Instrument Company in 1898, working his way up to become managing director. In offering his collection of instruments to the university, he stipulated that it should eventually be exhibited as a whole and be under the care of a paid curator. He also gave £3,300 to form the basis for a purchase fund for the museum. A selection of instruments was exhibited almost immediately after the announcement of the gift. In 1952 Whipple gave a further £500 to the museum, and after his death three years later the Vice-Chancellor was able to announce a bequest of some £20,000 (Cambridge University, 1956).

The generous benefaction of Whipple has enabled successive curators to develop and expand the collections by purchasing through the antique instrument market. The collections are displayed in the historic Free School, originally built in 1618 and extensively remodelled during the late nineteenth century to provide scientific laboratories. The building was adapted for museum use in the 1970s. The Whipple Museum boasts outstanding examples of instruments made by some of the best known and most skilful eighteenth-century instrument makers. There are also examples of nineteenth-century surveying equipment, and mathematical instruments of the nineteenth century and earlier.

At both these ancient universities, the collections of historic instruments form components of a broader enterprise for the study of the history of science. At Cambridge, the links between the collections and academic teaching are strongest; the Whipple's curator gives lectures and tutorials to students from the university's Department of the History of Science. Both the Whipple and the Museum of the History of Science in Oxford are very much museums for the antiquarian. They do not purport to offer a populist presentation of the history of science and do not offer information or display exhibits relating to modern science. They are museums of the art of the instrument maker, for the most part confining themselves to the period before the mass production of precision instruments, and avoiding the problems that collecting the material history of twentieth-century science presents. They have no real counterparts elsewhere in Britain. There are, however, comparable museums on the Continent, most notably in The Netherlands and in Italy, where rich collections present the experimental apparatus of the past.

3. Museums around the world

Museums, like any other aspect of culture, are products of the societies that beget them. They originated as forms of European cultural expression, and whilst there are similarities amongst museums in Britain, those in British colonies and museums on the Continent, there are also differences, just as there are differences between French, German and British societies. Do these national characteristics allow one to identify a particular museum as a product of the French, British or German *milieu?* Science and technology museums form the common thread across cultures for the institutions which we will compare in this chapter, but differences can be identified in the motives behind the founding of these institutions, in how each is funded, and in the way these museums present their messages to visitors.

France

The first museum to record and document technology and its artefacts was formed in France as part of the sweeping cultural changes which followed the revolution of 1789. In 1794 a Decree was passed by the government of the day, the National Convention, to set up an institution to be called the Conservatoire des Arts et Métiers which would form a public repository of machines, models, inventions, books and drawings (Richards, 1925, pp. 7–10). The Conservatoire was to be a national library of technology and crafts where visitors would learn how the machines worked and how they related to the industrial process. The suggestion was not new. In 1699 René Descartes, the celebrated philosopher, had outlined a similar scheme. In Descartes, museum-skilled craftsmen were to be attached to each set of exhibits to explain how each device worked and to answer visitors' questions.

The Conservatoire des Arts and Métiers opened five years after the government's Decree in the mediaeval Priory of Saint-Martin-des-Champs. Several collections of models, machines and scientific instruments were put on display. Some came from the inventor, Jacques Vaucanson, others from the Academie des Sciences. Over the nineteenth century the museum amassed large collections of valuable material, including Pascal's 1652 calculating machine, early photographic material, and huge numbers of scientific instruments. A massive library developed, providing an almost unique archive of science.

The museum seems not to have fulfilled the hopes of its founders in explaining technology and science to lay people. The collections were simply laid out for visitors to inspect. In 1925, Charles Richards observed that there was little or no explanatory material presented. Object labels were sparse, and the educational potential of the museum was not developed at all (Richards, 1925, p. 10). However, as Kenneth Hudson has observed, the Conservatoire was important in providing a precedent for collecting objects of a practical and technical nature (Hudson, 1987, p. 90). In post-revolutionary France, the Conservatoire represented the government's respect for culture not traditionally honoured in museums, and its aim to encourage practical arts and science and so to foster progress. It was no coincidence that the same year that the National Convention issued the Decree to set up the Conservatoire, a new school of applied science under state patronage opened. The Ecole Polytechnique became one of the premier scientific institutions of the nineteenth century. The Conservatoire was intended to explain science and technology to the public and so underline its importance for the development of the state.

A more recent Paris foundation has again taken contemporary science and technology as its theme. The Palais de la Découverte was established as an offshoot of an international exhibition in 1937 (Danilov, 1982, pp. 29–31). The original display was organised by the scientist Jean Perrin, and was intended to be temporary, but it proved so popular that it came to form the basis of a permanent exhibition. Like most other French cultural institutions, the Palais de la Découverte received most of its funds from the state. But it

Figure 3.1   A view of the entrance to Cité des Science et de l'Industrie at La
Villette, Paris. (Cité de Sciences et de l'Industrie, Paris.)

was not a rich organisation and it supplemented its state grant with
funds provided through industry.

The Palais de la Découverte never claimed to be a museum.
Collecting objects was not one of its aims. Rather, successive
generations of staff have sought to follow the objectives set by Jean
Perrin: 'to bring to everybody's attention the progress of science and
technology; to develop the scientific spirit and hence the qualities of
honest criticism, of free judgment' (Danilov, 1982, p. 30).
Experiments were demonstrated each day by university students
(Hudson, 1987, p. 103). Lectures, films, outreach programmes and
laboratory facilities were also offered to visitors. The greatest efforts
to stimulate interest in science were directed at the teenagers, again
following Perrin's aim 'to orient the young towards a career
corresponding to their capabilities and interests' (Danilov, 1982, p.
30).

During the 1980s the Palais de la Découverte became part of an
ambitious plan to establish a national science museum. The Cité des
Sciences et de l'Industrie which forms part of the La Villette
complex has cost the French government millions of francs since its

inception in 1979 (see Figure 3.1). Its initiation demonstrates the enhanced status enjoyed by science and technology during the 1980s. La Villette is a 'city-garden' complex developed from a derelict site, formerly one of the city's cattle markets. The complex is designed to provide a range of cultural opportunities, including an exhibition hall, pleasant gardens and a 'City of Music' which complements the 'City of Science and Industry'.

Many years of thought went into the organisation of the City of Science and Industry. It was decided from the outset that, although designated the national science museum, the displays would contain very few objects. Emphasis was to be on 'new interactive exhibit methods and advanced museum technology' (Cité des Sciences et de l'Industrie, 1986, p. 1). Maurice Levy, first president of the centre, identified two issues which should be addressed in exhibitions: the social impact of science and technology, and the decisions which confront us relating to science and technology in our everyday lives. Permanent exhibits included the geological history of the earth, human beings' relationship to their environment, the technology of transport and the psychology of language. There were displays aimed at older visitors, and young children were invited to explore technology for themselves in the discovery rooms or 'Inventorium' (Thomas, 1987). The museum opened its doors to the public in March 1986 (See Figure 3.1).

La Villette was intended to be more than just a leisure amenity for the capital city: within the City of Science and Industry there is an international conference centre; there is a research centre for the history of science, provided with funds to attract international scholars to work in Paris. The huge project has experienced teething problems; keeping such a vast range of interactive exhibits in action proved a mammoth maintenance job, and there were many adjustments to be made in the first years after opening. Nevertheless, La Villette complex has become an internationally important centre which has played its part in encouraging positive attitudes towards science and technology.

Germany

Although Germany is an international power of enormous stature with a large land mass and an enviable economic base, culturally it remains a federation of small states. In general, the federal government has little involvement in museums or other cultural institutions, and it is the local governments, or Länder, which provide much of the support for museums, art galleries and similar organisations. However, in the case of the Deutsches Museum (German Museum) in Munich, a unique partnership involving local and central governments and the commercial sector has evolved to create one of the most influential science and technology museums in the world.

The Deutsches Museum was the brainchild of a successful electrical engineer, Dr Oskar von Miller (Hudson, 1987, pp. 95–101). In 1903 he presented his ideas for a museum of science and technology to a meeting of government officials, academics and industrialists in Munich. His idea caught their imagination and won immediate support. Initially the museum was housed in the old building of the Bavarian National Museum. However, in 1911 the city of Munich decided to give the Deutsches Museum a site on an island in the River Isar, upon which could be constructed a suitable home for what was intended to be a celebration of German achievement in science and technology. Building work was completed within two years, and contributions to the cost were made by the City of Munich, the Bavarian state government, the German central government and German industry. German railways carried all the building materials free of charge, and the construction industry provided most of the materials at no cost and in many cases carried out the building work *gratis*.

Although the new building was ready for occupation in 1913, impending hostilities delayed the setting up of exhibits, and it was not until May 1925 that the museum was formally opened to the public (see Figure 3.2). Throughout the early years of the Deutsches Museum, its founder and first Director, Oskar von Miller, proved a tireless advocate and successful fundraiser. The museum received free heating and lighting from the City of Munich; universities seconded staff; money and help came from industry. The model he established, meshing together support from a variety of economic sources, has continued to serve the museum well. Representatives of local government, the Länder, and of the cities of Berlin, Bremen, Hamburg and Munich sit on the Supervisory Board together with academics, individuals nominated from professional and industrial associations, and representatives from major industrial companies. A

Figure 3.2   Visitors continue to flock to the Deutsches Museum in Munich, one
of the most influential museums of technology in the world.
(Deutsches Museum, Munich.)

separate Advisory Board also includes journalists from the technical
press, academics and industrialists. The close involvement of
German industry in the organisational structure of the museum has
ensured their continuing financial support and, perhaps as important, their help in kind. The Planetarium was set up in the 1920s
by Carl Zeiss of Jena and continues to be maintained by them.
Other companies provide similar technical support, and every year,
the museum receives gifts of technical equipment as well as publications relevant to the museum and its collections.

Exhibits within the museum are displayed to illustrate how science
and technology have developed (Deutsches Museum, 1988). Unsur-
prisingly, great emphasis is laid upon the achievements of German
individuals and organisations. Charles Richards, visiting the
museum shortly before its opening, was much impressed by the

overtly educational aims of the projects (Richards, 1925, p. 32). Many of the exhibits could be operated either by a guide or by the visitor pushing a button, and most important to him at least, the exhibits were arranged to illustrate change and, inevitably, progress.

From the beginning the museum was well received. By 1910 the museum had received over 300,000 visitors (Richards, 1925, p.30), many of them schoolchildren. In Munich, all pupils over ten years of age had to visit the museum once a year under the guidance of their teacher or a member of the museum staff. Public lectures were arranged in the evenings, and facilities for meetings and conferences offered to professional and academic societies. Von Miller was a skilled public relations operator and the Deutsches Museum became one of the most celebrated institutions of the late 1920s and 1930s. Its influence, particularly in the United States, was considerable. Since the end of the Second World War, although it has not enjoyed quite the same international prestige, the Deutsches Museum has nevertheless provided a superb example for museum professionals throughout the world, particularly in its tradition of presenting exhibits in working order and of demonstrating their operation.

The presentation of science and technology in the Deutsches Museum does suffer from certain limitations. The close involvement of German industry inhibits the development of exhibitions which critically examine the effects of industrial development on people. Technological progress is presented in very positive terms, stressing improvements in living standards and the economic success of innovation. The success of this German institution can be seen to some extent as a function of the strength of German industry. From the middle of the nineteenth century, Germany's commitment to technical education ensured the survival of its industries in increasingly competitive markets. The popularity and respect for the Deutsches Museum is part of that commitment – a recognition by German industry of the value of preserving and presenting to the public past achievements as a means of ensuring both due regard for scientists and technologists and a continuing and talented supply of new recruits.

North America

The pattern of museum development in the United States contrasts somewhat with that of Europe, In Europe, collections were first brought together by the great individual collectors of the seventeenth and eighteenth centuries, whereas the first institutions in the New World tended to be public museums, set up either by local governments or, more often, by societies and institutions such as universities.

Despite, or perhaps because of, this more recent history, the United States and Canada boast some of the most impressive and influential museums in the world. The premier museum (or rather network of museums) is the Smithsonian Institution in Washington, DC, whose foundation was made possible by a bequest from an Englishman who never set foot on United States soil. James Smithson, whose money established the Smithsonian, was born in 1765, the illegitimate son of the Duke of Northumberland and Elizabeth Macie. He pursued the life of a wealthy English gentleman interested in 'various branches of Natural Philosophy and particularly in Chemistry and Mineralogy' (Smithsonian Institution, 1983, p. 3). He became a Fellow of the Royal Society in 1787 and undertook a number of scientific investigations, mostly while residing on the Continent. Smithson died in 1829, leaving his estate to his nephew. The will stipulated that if the nephew subsequently died leaving no heirs, the balance of the legacy should pass 'to the United States of America, to found at Washington, under the name of the Smithsonian Institute, an establishment for the increase and diffusion of knowledge among men' (Smithsonian Institution, 1983, p. 3). The legacy did indeed pass to the USA on the death of Smithson's nephew in 1835. There followed lengthy debates within the government on how to interpret the terms of Smithson's will. Should the institution be a library, a school or university or even an experimental farm? The issue was resolved in 1846 when Congress established the Smithsonian Institution as a 'trust instrumentality of the United States responsible for research, the dissemination of academic findings and the administration of the National Collections' (Smithsonian Institution, 1983, p. 4). A Smithsonian Board of Regents, made up of the Chief Justice, the Vice President, three members of the Senate and nine citizen members, was established to administer the trust. The administrative head of the Institution, the Secretary, is elected by this Board of Regents. The original bequest still provides some funding for the institution. The remainder of its multimillion-dollar budget is made up of a combination of federal grants, gifts from individuals and organisations, and revenue from sales of its publications, income from shops and other visitor facilities.

The Smithsonian Institution is an enormous and complex organisation. Its constituent museums dominate the Mall in Washington which stretches down from Capitol Hill to the Lincoln Memorial. The Smithsonian's museums include: the National Museum of Natural History, the National Air and Space Museum, the Freer Gallery of Art, the Hirshhorn Museum and Sculpture Garden, and the National Museum of American History. Among these are some of the most visited museums in the world. Interestingly, there is no museum of science and technology in the list of Smithsonian museums. In 1964, what is now known as the National Museum of American History was built as the National Museum of History and Technology. The change in name during the 1970s reflects the nationalistic mission of the museum as well as its aim to record very broadly the development of the United States. Within the museum there is a Department of Science and Technology, and several important exhibitions illustrate scientific themes. These scientific themes are historically based, charting innovations in technologies such as communications and computers. Particular emphasis is given to social aspects of technological change. In the Information Age exhibition at the museum, the history of telephone systems is charted alongside the development of televisions and wartime code-cracking machines (Brown, 1991). How the technologies were used is demonstrated and explained through graphics, real exhibits, audio-visual presentations and interactive displays.

This particular exhibition contrasts strikingly with a museum further north in the US which concentrates entirely on information technology. The Computer Museum in Boston is based in a refurbished warehouse on the Boston waterfront. It was established in the early 1980s, largely on the initiative of the computer company DEC as a celebration of the achievements of electronic wizardry (The Computer Museum, 1985). The Computer Museum does contain a few historic exhibits, but the majority of its displays are made up of interactive exhibits using personal computers (Brown, 1991). The aim is to show the visitor what the technology is capable of, not how it came about. There is very little about the social or economic implications of the various forms of information technology.

The two exhibitions – the Information Age and the Computer Museum – illustrate the divide in North America between what are regarded as science museums which are primarily concerned with contemporary technology, and history museums which may be concerned with scientific or technical themes, but would not be labelled as science or technology museums because they deal with ideas and objects from the past. This tension between commemorating the past and displaying the present is evident in the development of another museum in the United States, the Chicago Museum of Science and Industry. The museum opened in 1933 largely as a result of the philanthropy of a local businessman, Charles Rosenwald, Chairman of Sears, Roebuck and Company. Rosenwald had visited the Deutsches Museum in 1911 with his eight-year-old son, whose delight in the exhibits encouraged the father to consider how such a museum could be brought to Chicago (Museum of Science and Industry, 1983). More than a decade later, Rosenwald got the backing of the influential Commercial Club of the city for the establishment of an 'industrial museum'. Before his death in 1932 Rosenwald was to provide the museum with $7 million dollars towards its exhibits.

Accommodation for the museum was available in the former Palace of Fine Arts, built for Chicago's 1893 World Columbian Exposition. The Palace had housed Chicago's natural history museum from 1894 until 1920, and the plaster, wood and glass structure was deteriorating rapidly, much to the dismay of local residents. The local government authority agreed to provide $5 million to restore the building with the understanding that the exterior would look exactly like it did in 1893, while the interior could be adapted to provide suitable facilities for a science and technology museum. The reconstruction of the building began in 1929, and four years later the museum opened to coincide with Chicago's World Fair. The Fair provided several of the museum's first exhibits including an oil rig, an oscilloscope, a stream turbine and a telephone exhibit.

Rosenwald wanted to create in Chicago a museum which would follow the Deutsches Museum and the London Science Museum in inspiring curiosity through exhibits which worked. Even more than in Munich or London, this principle became central to exhibit development from the very beginning. Displays were based on real objects which could be operated through a push button or demonstrated by a member of staff.

By 1940 the museum had run into serious difficulties. Rosenwald was no longer available to bale out the museum financially and the thirties had proved to be difficult economic times. A new President, Lenox Lohr, was charged with rescuing the museum from its doldrums and creating a viable financial entity. Lohr came to the museum from the National Broadcasting Company, and was very much the showman determined to convey the 'romance and drama and action' of science and technology (Museum of Science and Industry, 1983, pp. 14–18). He was determined to make the museum a more friendly place for visitors, and he commissioned new designers to make the exhibition halls more attractive. However, his most far-reaching innovation, which has shaped the subsequent character of the museum, was his invitation to industry to design and install exhibits. Sections of the museum are sponsored by commercial organisations; telecommunications has been sponsored and organised by the Bell Telephone System, and the 'Food for Life' exhibition was set up in the 1950s by Swift and Company.

The involvement of industry in this way has had certain consequences. The first is eclectic design styles; the museum has taken on the character of a trade fair rather than a uniformly planned exhibition. The second, as Kenneth Hudson has observed, is that the sponsor is identified with the particular branch of technology that their exhibit demonstrates, and the exhibit becomes a form of advertising for the company (Hudson, 1987, p. 105). Thirdly, the exhibitions are fundamentally uncritical; General Motors will not discuss disinterestedly the harmful environmental impact of the ever-increasing number of cars on the road. Innovation is presented as progress; technology invariably is said to serve to raise standards of living. As Hudson notes, 'the voice that comes out of the Museum of Science and Industry is unmistakably that of the Establishment' (Hudson, 1987, p. 106).

The exhibits developed at the Museum of Science and Industry since Lohr's days in the 1940s have concentrated increasingly on contemporary themes in science and technology and on participatory exhibits. That is not to say that history and objects have been banished completely. 'Yesterday's Main Street', a reconstruction of a 1910 Chicago street scene with its vintage cars and well-stocked shops, remains a popular exhibit. However, successive directors have tried to make the museum more of a contemporary science centre and less of a historical museum.

The education potential of the museum was further developed

from 1971 under the enthusiastic leadership of Victor Danilov, one of the leading protagonists of interactive science in the 1970s and 80s. Danilov saw the role of science centres as raising the scientific literacy of the public. He established a 'Science Education Center' to improve the services the museum provided for schools (Museum of Science and Industry, 1984), and he set up a science materials distribution service. Over the 1970s increasing emphasis was given to activities which could complement visits to the museum. Courses for teachers, field trips and summer camps were all successfully introduced. Under the present leadership of James Kahn, this emphasis on informal education continues, with a strong commitment to programmes intended to improve the general public's awareness of science and technology (Museum of Science and Industry, 1990).

Many museum professionals feel uneasy with the way in which sponsored exhibits have been allowed to develop at the Museum of Science and Industry. However, there can be no denying the museum's popularity. By 1973 attendances were up to the 3 million mark (Museum of Science and Industry, 1984). In the 1990s the museum anticipates annual figures in excess of 4 million. The Museum of Science and Industry does not charge for admission to the main galleries, but visitors are asked to pay for entry to certain major exhibitions such as the coal mine and the Omnimax theatre. In 1989 this revenue, together with income from other sales, provided nearly 40 per cent of the $25 million needed to operate the museum. Funds from the Chicago Park District, the State of Illinois and the federal government make up a further quarter of this budget; a further 10 per cent is provided through interest on investments, and the final portion is made up from a variety of sources: contributions and grants from companies and foundations, membership fees and education programme fees (Museum of Science and Industry, 1990).

The Museum of Science and Industry is structured as an independent, non-profit-making (in British parlance, charitable) organisation. There is a board of trustees, most of whom are drawn from the local and national business community. Corporations can subscribe to the annual membership scheme which gives certain privileges including use of certain private rooms for functions, and individuals can enrol as members and receive publications and free admission to certain exhibitions within the museum.

The close ties with the commercial world of Chicago, one of the United States' most important business communities, has laid rich foundations for the museum. In 1989, the market value of the museum's investments alone was $34,670,085 (Museum of Science and Industry, 1990). The museum seems to be able to entice almost any commercial organisation to give money, exhibitions or help. In its turn, the museum prides itself on operating like a business by putting the resources at its disposal to good use.

Conclusions

This brief review of museums from either side of the Atlantic demonstrates that museums of science and technology come in many shapes and forms. In terms of funding, it is fair to generalise that state support for cultural institutions tends to be strongest in France. In Germany, where the involvement of various levels of government was crucial to the gestation of the Deutsches Museum and where there is widespread recognition of the role of the state in supporting such institutions, funding has nevertheless developed in a more pluralistic manner. The close involvement of industry in the general operation of the organisation is recognised as an important component in the success of the Deutsches Museum.

In North America, the first museums tended to be publicly funded organisations, but the pattern of development over the twentieth century has tended to follow the German model. Most museums in the United States and many in Canada are structured as non-profit-making bodies with boards of trustees carrying responsibility for finances and general management. There are also *very* generous tax incentives, so it makes sense for companies to contribute; not so in Britain. Museums in the US have been particularly successful in harnessing the support of businesses through membership schemes and through the sponsorship of exhibitions. Not all museums follow the Chicago policy of allowing sponsors to install exhibitions developed and designed entirely outside the museum. However, money from the commercial sector is crucial to the capital programmes of most North American institutions.

The museum field in Britain is particularly complicated. The tradition of public museums funded by state provision which became increasingly common from the mid nineteenth century has been overlain in the last twenty years by an increasing number of museums adopting the North American model of independent trust structure, allowing for plurality of funding. Some institutions in Britain, like Chicago in the US, receive a fair proportion of their operating funds from state coffers. Others on both sides of the Atlantic are dependent on admission fees and other sources of earned income.

In terms of presentation, the museums reviewed in this chapter have developed particular styles. The Chicago Museum of Science and Industry began by following the Deutsches Museum in concentrating on working models and exhibits. The artefacts of technology were paramount and formed the major focus for both museums. The French, both in the Palais de la Découverte and the Centre for Science and Industry at La Villette, have stressed the interactive approach, providing informal learning experiences for their visitors by encouraging them to do, rather than simply observe, and since the 1970s the Chicago museum has worked hard to place itself in this category also. It seems that national styles have been passed on across geographical boundaries, and in some cases have turned full circle. Museums in North America seem least comfortable in blending the past with the present in their displays. Past achievements are perceived as history rather than science. Perhaps this attitude reflects a broader culture in which progress is based on the development of contemporary practice with little value given to historical perspective.

Victor Danilov has reviewed the development of science museums around the world and has divided the kinds of styles we have identified into phases (Danilov, 1982, pp. 17–41). Phase One museums are those like the original Science Museum in London or the Conservatoire des Arts et Métiers which simply collect historical material. Museums of Phase Two include the Deutsches Museum and concentrate still on the past, but seek to bring historical exhibits to life by using working machinery. Phase Three museums place little emphasis on collections of historic objects and instead concentrate on participatory exhibits stressing contemporary themes. Kenneth Hudson, reviewing *Museums of Influence*, identifies a further more recent phase – that of museums which seek to place science and technology in their social context (Hudson, 1987, pp. 108–12). The first of these, and one which has exerted enormous influence in Hudson's opinion, is the Municipal Museum at Rüsselsheim in

Germany (Schirmbeck, 1981). Rüsselsheim is the home of the Opel car manufacturing organisation, and the museum could easily have become simply a storehouse for the evolution of the various technologies in which Opel have been involved. Instead, it has sought to interweave exhibits showing Adam Opel's beginnings in sewing machine technology, his later efforts in motorcycle manufacturing and his first offerings as a car manufacturer, alongside material depicting what life was like for those working in the factory at various periods in the company's history, and what had been the effects on the town of the introduction of mass production techniques and modern technology. The displays do not pull their punches. The unpleasant social aspects of industrialisation, the involvement of Opel with National Socialism in the 1930s, providing armoured cars for the Nazi's re-armament programme, are all displayed unequivocally.

Hudson believes that the intimate involvement of commercial organisations with museums such as the Deutsches Museum in Munich or the Museum of Science and Industry in Chicago makes the possibility of developing such socially aware displays negligible. They require instead a degree of political freedom and, of course, the financial support to make displays possible. Hudson does not rule out commercial organisations as the providers of that support; the crucial point is the structuring of the relationship between industry and museums. Commercial money for developments has continued to be important in the 1980s and 1990s, but more museums are taking the Rüsselsheim approach of interweaving the technical with the social and looking squarely at technological change in the broadest possible terms. Those museums are managing the relationship with their financial benefactors in ways different to the model developed first by Oskar von Miller in Germany. As we shall see in the next chapter, that new approach owes much, in Britain at least, to the growing interest in industrial archeology, which has tended to take a social rather than a nuts-and-bolts approach to the history of technology.

4. The heritage phenomenon

In the late 1980s it was estimated that in the UK, at least one museum opened every fortnight (Hewison, 1987, p. 9). To some this statistic seemed not only astonishing, but alarming. To others, it indicated that the heritage business was simply booming. Many of these new museums are independent museums, usually set up as charitable companies – that is, registered both as non-profit-making organisations and as companies limited by guarantee. Their day-to-day operations are often funded by entrance charges. Capital developments are financed by sponsorship or by donations from charitable foundations. Their growth since the 1970s has proved enormously influential, changing the way all museums operate and relate to their visitors. Many of these new museum projects are concerned with industrial archeology, including technology and transport (Prince and McLoughlin, 1987, p. 26). In this chapter we will focus in detail on several of these 'heritage' projects and discuss their implications for the presentation of science and technology in museums.

I am not going to try and define too closely what is meant by the term 'heritage'. It is certainly something distinct from 'history' or 'historic'. 'Heritage' seems to embody notions of nostalgia for times lost, and the imperative for preservation. However, leaving aside for the moment the problems of definition, let us first review the background to the very phenomenon itself.

Industrial archeology

The emergence of the heritage industry has been much bound up with increasing interest in 'industrial archeology', a term first used in 1955 to refer to the study of the material remains of Britain's declining industrial past (Ironbridge Gorge Museum, 1991, p. 1). Initially, the focus was on transport: the defunct canal system and the ever-decreasing British railway network. Interest quickly spread to other industries undergoing change and decline. A national society, the Association for Industrial Archeology, was set up in the early 1960s. Academic courses are now offered and there are many learned and popular tomes on the subject.

Enthusiasm for industrial archeology derives from concern about preserving links with a fast disappearing way of life. That interest has mushroomed in the 1970s and 1980s is understandable primarily in terms of the enormous social and economic changes western industrialised society has undergone. Industries upon which Britain traditionally based her prosperity such as coal, iron and steel and textiles, have either virtually disappeared or have changed out of all recognition in their patterns of work. Discovering and preserving relics from such industries helps provide a sense of continuity and identity for towns and localities fast losing their primary economic base.

One project undertaken by these early enthusiasts for preserving industrial remains was the rescue of the old iron furnace at Coalbrookdale in Shropshire (Smith, 1989). The Coalbrookdale Museum and Furnace Site opened in October 1959. It provided a nucleus for volunteer work during the 1960s and identified significant industrial remains in the Ironbridge and Coalbrookdale area. The idea of setting up a museum based on these industrial remains was mooted in 1967 by the Development Corporation of the new town of Dawley, set up in 1964 as an attempt to revitalise the increasingly derelict Shropshire coalfield. Dawley was subsequently renamed Telford, and a multiple-site museum based on the Ironbridge Gorge was planned to ensure the continued enhancement and maintenance of the environment surrounding Telford New Town. It would provide a cultural amenity, making the town more attractive to industrial investors and a more interesting home for those settling in the area. As we shall see, in motivational terms the Ironbridge project foreshadowed many of the urban renewal programmes spearheaded by Michael Heseltine during the 1980s.

The museum that Dawley Development Corporation envisaged was to be an independent body, ultimately reliant on visitor income to fund its day-to-day operations. A development trust was established to raise capital for the various programmes which would be needed to bring the project to life. The Corporation wanted to see local people involved, and a strong Friends organisation was set up. In 1967 these ideas were relatively new to the British museum world, dominated by the network of local authority museums based in civic buildings in town centres. But perhaps the most innovative feature of the Ironbridge Museum was the absence of buildings themselves, for the founders of Ironbridge Museum wanted to pursue a very different tradition, that of the open air museums of northern Europe. Ironbridge Museum was to be based on a multiplicity of sites relating to the original industries of the Gorge.

In 1968 a museum trust was established, and soon after that a £1 million appeal was launched to save Ironbridge. During the subsequent two years volunteers identified possible exhibits, cleared sites and generally undertook the burden of the project. In 1971, on advice from the Museums Association, the Trust appointed Ironbridge's first director, Neil Cossons, later to become director of the London Science Museum. In Spring 1972, a curator of technology was also appointed, Stuart Smith. Further support staff were also taken on the payroll, enabling the project to be put on a more professional footing and sites to be prepared for regular opening to the public.

The first main objective was to develop the Blists Hill site. Although much remained to be completed, the site was opened to the public for a minimal charge in 1973. In 1972 work had begun on restoring the Iron Bridge, the central feature of the gorge which provided a distinctive unifying symbol for the museum itself (see Figure 4.1). By 1974 this work was completed and was complemented by further restoration to the Toll House on the bridge, which continues to provide an information point and small shop. In 1976 the Coalport China Works Museum was opened. The following year, Ironbridge was awarded the first of many accolades to come when it became the Museum of the Year. All the resultant publicity gave a great fillip to visitor figures. The following year further success came when Ironbridge became the first European Museum of the Year. By the 1980s, Ironbridge was well established on a number of sites: Blists Hill, Coalport China Museum, Jackfield Tile Museum (opened in 1985), the Museum of Iron (opened in 1979), successor to the Coalbrookdale Museum, Rosehill House (the

Figure 4.1 Thomas Telford's Ironbridge forms the centrepiece for the Ironbridge Gorge Museum. (Ironbridge Gorge Museum, Telford.)

former home of one of Abraham Darby's family) and the Museum of the River (opened in 1989) (see Figures 4.2 and 4.3).

Ironbridge became an academic centre through the Institute of Industrial Archeology, set up jointly with the University of Birmingham in 1981. The Institute initially offered diploma courses for postgraduate students as well as short courses for practising professionals. In 1987 it became the Ironbridge Institute and began offering courses in Heritage Management. Research programmes have been undertaken by Institute staff, and archeology projects have been undertaken through the funding of the Manpower Services Commission.

There can be no denying the success of Ironbridge Museum. In 1988, the complex attracted 404,000 visitors (Ironbridge Gorge Museum, 1991). The gorge is now an attractive rural environment. This has been achieved through massive capital investment, some

Figure 4.2   The trade showroom, Jackfield Tile Museum, Ironbridge.
(Ironbridge Gorge Museum, Telford.)

provided by Telford Development Corporation and some by
industrial partners. Visitor income supports a large staff complement. Grant income has enabled a vigorous educational programme
to flourish, providing training courses for teachers as well as
materials for children to use. Ambitious plans for further development during the 1990s include a new Museum of Industrialisation
as well as the expansion of existing sites and the development of
tourist accommodation aimed at providing a complete package for
visitors.

Ironbridge is a museum about industry. Although many of its
most important exhibits, including the furnace at Coalbrookdale, the
Museum of Iron and the wrought ironworks at Blists Hill could be
classified as technology, it is not a science museum. Displays do
contain technical details about the industries, such as the development of iron making, but the main aim of the exhibitions is to
explain the social and economic reasons behind the developments.

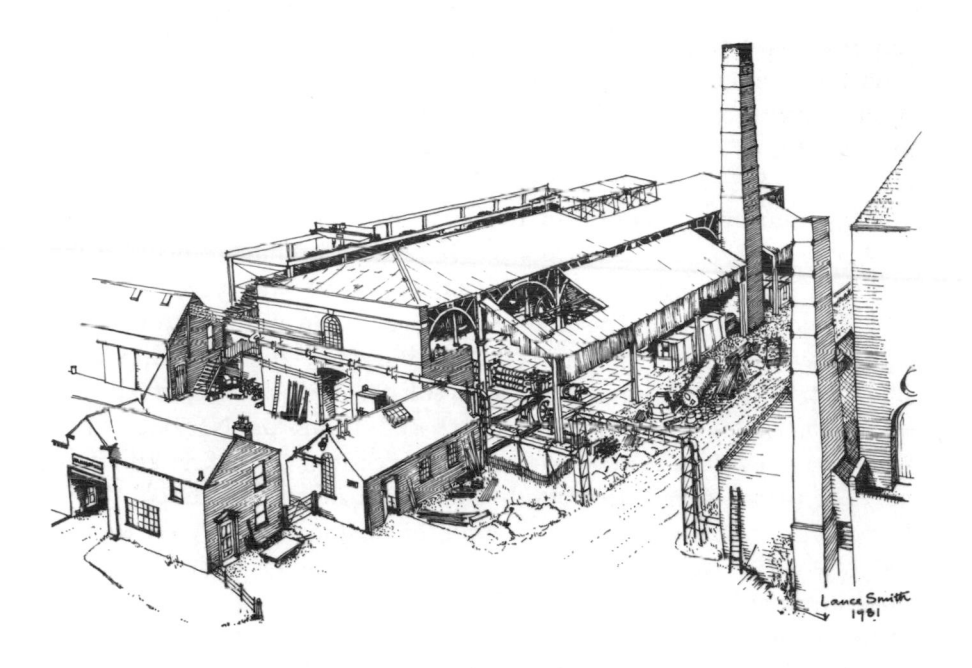

Figure 4.3 The Wrought Ironworks, Blists Hill, reconstructed and developed entirely by MSC labour for Ironbridge Gorge Museum. (Ironbridge Gorge Museum, Telford.)

With its roots in the tradition of open air museums, Ironbridge is a folk museum providing visitors with a picture of a past way of life. At Blists Hill, by far the most popular of the museum's sites, visitors are invited to become part of a Victorian street of about 1890. Demonstrators in period costume bake bread, make candles, sell sweets and serve food in a Victoria pub. Visitors can walk into a doctor's house and see what an estate office would have been like. The ironworks are in operation allowing visitors to watch the process of wrought iron production. How much visitors learn about life in the 1890s is debatable; inevitably, the information conveyed through the exhibits is incomplete and rather shallow. However, most visitors enjoy the theatrical spectacle and many return time and again. Ironbridge's success has been to strike the right popular note in its museum presentations, providing academic material through other means such as the Ironbridge Institute's courses and publications.

Ironbridge, through its success in attracting both visitors and funding, has provided an example to many other independent museums which have followed it. It was not, however, the only project during the 1970s to take up the idea of establishing an open air museum focusing on the everyday life of yesteryear. From the late 1950s, Frank Atkinson, then Director of the Bowes Museum in County Durham, recognised the pace of social change the North East was beginning to experience. He began to publicise his idea for a museum to record the daily life of the region and to collect from the public a wide variety of objects which could eventually be used in displays (Allan, 1991, pp. 4–5). By the late sixties the support of Durham County Council had been enlisted and Beamish Hall and some 300 acres of land were purchased from the National Coal Board to provide a site for the museum. Visitors were first admitted in 1972 to see a restored smithy and a small row of shops. As at Ironbridge, putting together exhibits to demonstrate a past way of life often involved dismantling and reassembling large pieces of machinery such as a large winding engine and a gas works. The museum now includes working passenger locomotives operating from a reconstructed station, as well as period sets making up a 'town' allowing visitors to see offices and shops of times gone by. A tramway system provides transport along the main street of the town (Harris, Lawson and Price, n.d.). Like Ironbridge, Beamish does not set out to explain technology or how it developed. But it does provide a context for industry, showing the social and economic background to life in the North East in its industrial heyday.

Renewal of the urban environment

During the 1970s, Britain's serious economic problems were countered by far-reaching changes to industry and work practices. The precarious boom years of the 1960s when the British people had 'never had it so good' culminated in the spiralling inflation and high wage demands of the early 1970s. Since the mid-1970s successive British governments' primary economic objective has been to keep inflation in check. In the 1970s the means of getting inflation under control were stringent measures resulting in very high unemployment. The government's panacea for the unemployed, and particularly the young unemployed, was the establishment of the

Manpower Services Commission (MSC) under the auspices of the Department of Employment whose brief it was to create jobs for the unemployed. Throughout the country, museums and other projects involving the conservation of historic buildings benefited enormously from Manpower Services Commission schemes. In some cases, the only paid staff were MSC-funded.

High unemployment in the late 1970s and early 1980s was particularly widespread in areas associated with traditional heavy industry such as coal and engineering. This provided for museums the large pool of skilled labour needed to rescue, restore and operate the obsolete machinery of industries now past. At Ironbridge, the construction of the Wrought Ironworks was carried out entirely by MSC-funded workers (Smith, 1989). Many textile workers – both engineers and operatives – found new employment in museums such as Helmshore in Lancashire, Styal Mill in Cheshire and Trencherfield Mill at Wigan. The decline of traditional heavy industries took its toll in many of Britain's cities. None suffered more so than Liverpool, whose economic problems dated back to the decline of international shipping in the 1960s and culminated in the Toxteth riots of 1981. Riots in Liverpool were followed by unrest in other major cities including Manchester and Bristol. The government's response to the social problems of these cities was to set up and finance programmes to encourage urban renewal.

In 1982, Michael Heseltine, Secretary of State for the Environment, personally oversaw the setting up of the Urban Development Grant Programme, intended to inject capital into projects which would improve inner-city environments. In Merseyside, the first Development Corporation was set up to support and initiate projects which would mitigate some of Liverpool's severe problems. One of the Corporation's first actions was to agree to develop the Albert Dock to house the Merseyside Maritime Museum and provide a home for an outstation of the Tate Gallery. The Albert Dock is a stunning architectural attraction with magnificent warehouses on a waterfront location. £2.25 million was spent on buildings for the Maritime Museum; the Tate cost a further £2 million (Hewison, 1987, p. 100). This investment has created for Liverpool an enclave of heritage offering visitors a museum, an art gallery and the exclusive boutiques which form part of the dock complex.

In other cities, museums similarly played an important role in urban renewal programmes during the 1980s. In Manchester, for example, the metropolitan authority, the Greater Manchester Council (GMC) undertook the refurbishment of Liverpool Road Station to provide a home for a museum of science and industry. It was one of a number of projects to restore dilapidated industrial buildings in which the Council played a major role. Liverpool Road Station was the terminus of the first passenger railway established in 1830 between Manchester and Liverpool. From the 1840s, the station ceased to be used for passengers and became principally a goods depot. However, the original buildings survived virtually intact until the station closed in the mid-1970s. By 1980 the site was in a state of almost total dereliction, but for railway enthusiasts Liverpool Road Station was an important, even sacrosanct site, and they enlisted the financial support of the Greater Manchester Council to stage celebrations for the 150th anniversary of the opening of the Liverpool and Manchester Railway. The celebrations were a great success and the Council were persuaded to take on the task of restoring the site and establishing there a museum about Manchester's distinguished industrial past (Kennedy, 1987).

The Council were already associated with a museum of science and technology, part of UMIST, the city's technological university. In the late 1960s Donald Cardwell, then Reader in the History of Science at UMIST and one of the country's leading historians of science, had managed to win support within UMIST to bring together exhibits illustrating the history of engineering and science of the North West. Throughout the 1970s, Richard Hills, the museum's Director, collected textile machines, steam engines, gas engines and exhibits about paper making and printing. The museum followed the earlier traditions of the Deutsches Museum, becoming one of a new breed of working museums. Staff constraints meant that machines could not be operated every day, but on one weekend per month the majesty of north-western engineering was put in motion for all to see. The principle of restoring exhibits to working order and then demonstrating them in action to the public was one which became especially important when the museum was transferred to the Liverpool Road site, becoming the Greater Manchester Museum of Science and Industry.

By the late 1970s, the museum's accommodation on the UMIST campus had become cramped and inadequate. The GMC were by then involved in providing financial support through its Recreation and Arts committee. A move to Liverpool Road Station and the

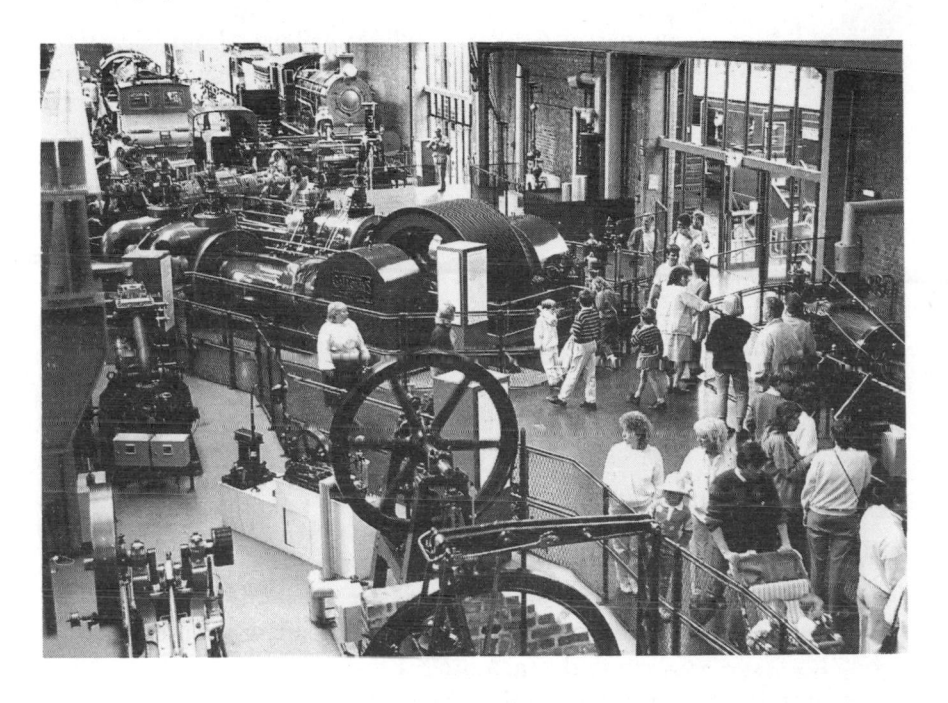

Figure 4.4   The Power Hall, Museum of Science and Industry, Manchester, the
first part of the museum to open in 1983. (Museum of Science and
Industry, Manchester.)

transfer of the collections to a new body, the Greater Manchester
Museum of Science and Industry Trust, provided scope for further
development. The exhibits in store provided the basis for new
displays which could be set up relatively quickly. By establishing a
charitable trust, bodies such as UMIST could remain involved with
the project while passing on financial responsibility to the GMC.

The first phase of the museum opened in September 1983 on the
Castlefield site. The station buildings themselves were restored and
housed a temporary exhibition provided by the Deutsches Museum
as well as a display explaining some of the history behind the Liverpool to Manchester Railway. A former goods shed provided exhibition space for a display of motive power with working steam engines
and gas engines. This Power Hall still forms an impressive centrepiece for the museum where visitors can view the achievements of
the pioneers of the Industrial Revolution (see Figure 4.4).

All the buildings which formed the original station complex
required restoration. Exhibitions opened phase by phase as funds

and building work permitted. In 1986 a gallery about electricity generation opened in two restored bays of the original station warehouse. That year, the museum also accepted responsibility for the neighbouring Air and Space Museum set up three years previously by Manchester City Council. In 1988, several further sections of the museum opened with Underground Manchester, and Xperiment!, an interactive science centre. The museum claims to be the fastest growing museum in Europe. New exhibitions have continued to open with impressive regularity. In 1990, a gallery about the exploration of space, 'Out of this World', brought interactive technology into the former Air and Space Museum. The following year, The Gas Gallery, an exhibition charting the history of gas power opened, complementing the displays about electrical power generation nearby.

During the 1980s Liverpool Road Station was transformed from a decaying eyesore into one of the showpieces of Manchester. Building work alone has cost millions of pounds; funds were initially provided through the metropolitan authority, but other public sector agencies have contributed, including English Heritage, the Urban Programme and, more recently, the Central Manchester Development Corporation. The success of the enterprise has brought many awards, including the Museum of the Year award in 1990. It has attracted many visitors: in 1987/8, there were approximately 280,000 visitors. By 1994, the museum predicts that over 400,000 people will pass through its turnstiles (Museum of Science and Industry, 1991, p. 11). Visitor figures are crucial to the finances of the museum; admission charges were introduced in 1987 providing additional cash to fund further developments.

Arguments for the economic benefits which accrue from projects like this have been well rehearsed. The museum itself becomes an important employer, often in an area such as Manchester where all new jobs are welcome. The local building trade gains lucrative contracts for prestigious and satisfying work. The museum becomes a customer for design services in the development of its displays, and the visitors themselves become valuable customers not only for the retail outlets within the museum, but also for local traders. In Castlefield, the Museum of Science and Industry can also claim credit for encouraging its neighbour, Granada Television, to invest substantial capital sums in a new visitor attraction, 'Granada Studios Tours'.

However, the balance sheet is a complicated one. Museums such as this, offering carefully researched displays presented to the highest possible design standards, have enormous running costs. In 1991/2, the museum forecast operating expenditures in excess of £2 million (Museum of Science and Industry, 1991, p. 21). 87 per cent of those costs will be provided by central government, through the Office of Arts and Libraries, which assumed financial responsibility for the museum following the abolition of the metropolitan authorities in 1986.

The benefits to the community of projects such as that at Castlefield, or the many other heritage projects which have been undertaken as part of urban renewal programmes, cannot be measured entirely in financial terms. The development of a visitor attraction in Wigan based at 'Wigan Pier' has revitalised a formerly depressed and depressing area into an astonishingly popular attraction, helping to change people's image of the town (see Figure 4.5). Enhancing urban landscapes through the careful use of historic buildings, not just for museum purposes but for shop developments, offices and residential purposes has proved one of the success stories of the 1980s, reversing urban decline and breathing life into urban industrial areas again. In Manchester the metropolitan council was a prime mover in the restoration of Central Station, formerly one of the main passenger termini in the city, into an exhibition hall, G-Mex. Like Liverpool Road Station, Central Station has been transformed from a decaying wreck into a landmark.

The regeneration of inner city areas through heritage developments has proved an important strategy in North American cities also. In Baltimore, for example, the harbour has been rebuilt to provide a site for several cultural and leisure developments including the Maryland Science Centre and a magnificent aquarium which attracts more than 1 million visitors a year. The city's museums and art galleries provide a cultural base for the town, helping to attract new investment to replace lost industries. In Toronto, warehouses on the lake shore have provided accommodation for shops and art exhibitions. In New York, South Street Seaport links shopping with museums in a multimillion-dollar development designed to attract visitors with a mix of culture and commercialism.

Figure 4.5   Wigan Pier Heritage Centre. The day out includes a canal trip from
one display across to Trencherfield Mill. (Wigan Pier Heritage
Centre.)

Conspicuous consumption

The success of heritage attractions since the 1970s cannot be attributed only to interest in industrial history. Pride in historic buildings and the heritage of suburban and rural environments has become increasingly widespread over the past two decades. In 1967 the first four Conservation Areas were designated as areas of special architectural or historic interest which should be developed with appropriate care. By 1975, only eight years later, there were 3,264 such areas throughout Britain. By 1984, the figure had risen to 5,194 (Feist and Hutchison, 1989, p. 74). Since, the mid-1970s membership of the National Trust, one of the country's largest landowners and custodian of many of the nation's finest country houses, has been growing rapidly. Between 1984 and 1989, 2,000 new members joined each week, By 1988, the National Trust had a staggering 1,664,000 members all prepared to pay an annual subscription towards the upkeep of houses and land constituting the nation's heritage. Similarly, English Heritage, formed in 1983, launched its own membership scheme and by 1988 had approximately 200,000 members (Feist and Hutchison, 1989, p. 69).

The widespread interest in historic buildings and the enthusiasm for preserving the past are part of an effort to provide the stability that notions of history can sometimes engender. This function of heritage is particularly important during times of fast social, technological and economical change. The success of organisations such as the National Trust, English Heritage and the numerous Friends organisations run by museums throughout the country also reflects the increasing leisure time that many people have experienced during the 1980s; increasing prosperity has created a market for tourist attractions offering a day's family entertainment.

Heritage versus history

The heritage industry has excited a great deal of debate. Robert Hewison's carefully argued thesis in *The Heritage Industry*, published in 1987, suggested that museums and heritage centres had become economic panaceas, replacing lost industries with new employment and somehow inhibiting the development of different kinds of technologies and alternative economic strategies. There can be no dispute that museums such as Beamish and Ironbridge have become major employers in areas which have suffered severe economic decline. There is surely nothing intrinsically wrong in this: tourism and culture are as valid sources of income for a region as any other service industry.

Hewison's more worrying criticism concerns the displays and period sets presented within these heritage attractions. He argues persuasively that they cannot be regarded as 'historic' in the sense of offering a true glimpse of the past but instead present a comforting, partial reconstruction of a rather indeterminate yesteryear, representing the 'dreamlands' of the museum curator or designer. Hewison suggests that museums' concern to make their 'product', heritage, easily accessible to all affords little credit to their visitors' capacity to appraise critically more exhaustive historical material. He points to the similarity between attractions – a reconstructed Ironbridge scene being in essence the kind of set which could be used at Beamish or the Black Country Museum or Wigan Pier. He asserts that such presentations of history dull rather than excite the imagination making impossible visitors' more personal reconstructions of the past. Such comments must be taken seriously by curators and designers (Hewison, 1987, pp. 139–44). Are museums in the business of marketing nostalgia based on the sentimentality of a cosy comforting image of times-gone-by? Or are there broader aims underlying the cute costumes of staff and the olde worlde products for sale?

Museum professionals, including Peter Lewis, Director of Beamish, have taken grave exception to Hewison's comments. They argue that their displays help stimulate memories and arouse curiosity in the past. Sometimes that curiosity stems from wondering at the magnificence of a steam engine, sometimes from realising the horror of the primitive conditions of the Victorian working classes, and sometimes from participating in a Victorian school lesson (Lewis, 1991). Hewison draws little distinction between museums such as Ironbridge or Beamish and heritage centres such as Wigan Pier. Museum professionals such as Stephen Feber, Director of Styal Mill are quick to emphasise the distinction pointing to the authenticity of museum buildings and collections in contrast to the artifice and theatrical nature of heritage centres.

Although there can be no denying the success of museums during the 1980s in attracting huge numbers of visitors, there is evidence that the heritage industry is in decline. A recent report indicates that average attendances per museum fell over the 1980s. The problem of shrinking visitor numbers affects small museums, many of which are dependent on income from admission charges. Since 1988 the Manpower Services Commission has been reorganised into the Training Commission, and the schemes which provided so many museums with valuable cheap labour have disappeared. In 1989 Tourist Board grants were stopped in England and Wales, removing another potential source of important development capital. There is a real danger that the 1990s will see many museum projects go bankrupt. Part of the problem seems to be 'market saturation'. Another is competition from attractions offering not history or even heritage, but 'visitor experiences'. These include Granada Studios Tours, Alton Towers and Derbyshire's American Adventure Theme Park.

Others have suggested that the problem is not so much accessibility, as the reverse – an absence or at least a retreat of scholarship. Museums should recognise the priceless resource that they offer the public in their collections and encourage ways of presenting their exhibits which will challenge visitors to use their own imaginations to investigate the past. Hewison warns that the business life for 'heritage' may be short. Middleton observes that over-supply is a normal occurrence during rapid market growth; the efficient survive, and the inefficient are taken over or die. Hewison's advice to museums in such a competitive field is to make sure that what is on offer to the public arouses and satisfies intellectual curiosity and does not merely pander to the passing whims of marketing fashion.

The heritage of science and technology

What effects have the heritage industry had on the presentation of science and technology? Technology has certainly become a much more common subject for museums to present, as many of the new museums of the 1980s were based on an industry or industries in decline. For example, the Big Pit Museum in Gwent was set up following the closure of the colliery by British Coal; Queen's Mill in Burnley opened as a museum shortly after the commercial production of cloth ceased. In developments like these, technology is

Figure 4.6   Gossage's soap displayed at Catalyst, a museum set up in the
              headquarters of the soap manufacturer at Widnes. (Catalyst,
              Widnes.)

presented very clearly in context, its application forming the very
basis for the museum.

Market forces have certainly brought changes which have forced
curators and designers to make the technical aspects of exhibitions
more accessible, and it is now accepted that a design brief about a
technical subject should have a social and economic dimension. For
example, the Babbage exhibition, which opened in 1991 at the
Science Museum, includes a full-scale reconstruction of Charles
Babbage's Difference Engine; the exhibit is supported by panels
giving details of the principal characters in the Babbage story. This
more populist approach underlies the efforts to provide visitors with
exhibitions which will not be too intimidating and which will capture
the attention of children. The development of hands-on science
centres as part of some industrial heritage projects has provided this

Figure 4.7 A computer information station on Scientrific!, Catalyst's hands-on
gallery. (Catalyst, Widnes.)

popular appeal. For example, in Nottingham at the home of the
mathematician George Green (1793–1841), a windmill was restored
to working order during the 1980s. Green is not a particularly
famous figure in the history of science despite the importance of the
theorems he suggested in the 1820s and 1830s. His family owned the
windmill which he managed for much of his working life and where
he wrote some of his scientific papers. During the 1970s the mill, by
then derelict, was threatened with demolition. A local group,
anxious that George Green's achievements should be commemor-
ated, was formed, and following petitions to the local council, the
site was acquired and restoration work begun (Tait, 1989, pp. 89–
92). By 1986, the mill was in working order again, grinding flour.
In the outbuildings there was space to tell Green's story and explain
some of the mathematics. However, Green left behind few material
possessions. There are no papers, not even a portrait. Moreover, his

mathematics is extremely esoteric to those of us unskilled beyond school arithmetic. Instead of a more conventional display, a hands-on science display was set up to convey to visitors some of the background to Green as an explorer of natural phenomena. The approach proved popular, and in 1988, only a year after opening, the mill received 60,000 visitors – a considerable achievement for a modest out-of-town attraction.

In Widnes, Catalyst, a project based in the historic Gossage's soap factory on the banks of the Mersey estuary, has involved the local council and many industrial chemical companies in setting up a museum explaining the background to the chemical industry (see Figure 4.6). The development of the museum has involved considerable renovation of the building, and the council have put much effort into reclaiming the derelict surrounding area to create a pleasant recreational facility including waterside industrial trails. Catalyst's second phase, which opened in 1991, was an interactive gallery called Scientrific!, offering visitors hands-on experience of certain chemical processes and products (see Figure 4.7).

How much of the heritage industry will survive the 1990s remains to be seen. However, there can be no doubt that museums such as Ironbridge, Beamish, the Maritime Museum in Liverpool and the Museum of Science and Industry in Manchester have enhanced the local landscape, have encouraged a new generation of museum visitors who no longer think of a museum as a dark, dusty institution where no-one speaks, and have helped present the human dimension of many forms of science and technology.

5.   *Uncommon classrooms*

The Science Museum in London was developed in the 1870s as a centre for the promotion of excellence in science and technology education. Educational inspiration was its task. It pursued this goal in the twentieth century by becoming a repository for past scientific achievements, a museum in the sense of preserving the past through collecting historic objects. By the 1920s, visitors could view the apparatus of science and the products of technology, but they had a fairly passive experience, seeing objects which were all carefully labelled, but not touching or doing. In the 1930s, the Children's Gallery provided exhibits to stimulate the curiosity of visitors (Hartley, 1938); these exhibits were intended to be touched and used. This hands-on approach, together with the development of working exhibits which could be turned on by a button or a handle, set an important example to educationalists in North America in the 1960s who set out to create new kinds of science museums where people would do, rather than look, and where the emphasis would not be on collecting objects, but on communicating ideas.

The two most influential institutions in the development of these hands-on science museums or science centres have undoubtedly been the Exploratorium in San Francisco, and the Ontario Science Centre in Toronto. Both were set up in the late 1960s, developing very different and very distinctive styles. Both have provided inspiration to others throughout the world. We will begin our review of science centres by looking at these two innovative museums and then examining how they have influenced projects elsewhere.

The Exploratorium, San Francisco

The Exploratorium is the brain-child of the late Dr Frank

77

Oppenheimer (1912–1985). Oppenheimer was an atomic physicist by training and a philosopher and humanist by nature; he believed that exploring the natural world was as much the province of the artist as the scientist. Through the Exploratorium he was able to share his fascination for the phenomena of nature with hundreds of thousands of people.

During the Second World War, Oppenheimer worked with his brother, Robert, on the Manhattan project, developing the atom bomb which devastated Hiroshima and Nagasaki in 1945 (Hein, 1990, pp. 7–15). In the 1950s his pre-war association with the Communist Party resulted in blacklisting, and he found himself unable to secure a post in a university. In order to earn a livelihood he pursued such diverse occupations as cattle ranching and school teaching. In this latter occupation he became fascinated by the problem of how to allow children to experience scientific concepts such as pressure, temperature or the polarisation of light, so he developed classroom demonstrations which allowed his pupils to feel effects and to acquire new dimensions of understanding. In 1959 he returned to university life when he accepted a post in the physics department at the University of Colorado, but he continued to be interested in the communication of ideas through demonstrations and activities. In 1965 he was awarded a Guggenheim travelling fellowship to visit Europe to study the history of twentieth-century physics and to work at University College, London. At the same time he visited many science museums throughout Europe. He returned to the USA greatly impressed by the Children's Gallery at the Science Museum in London and by other institutions such as the Deutsches Museum in Munich. He became convinced that America needed such an institution to bring science to a wide audience, making concepts accessible and understandable.

Oppenheimer developed a framework of ideas for his new science museum around which the exhibits were planned. The aim was for visitors to be able to touch and use the exhibits, to explore the natural world for themselves. In November 1968 he published *A Rationale for a Science Museum* suggesting the psychology of perception as an organising principle for the exhibits (Oppenheimer, 1968). He went on to outline five main sections based on hearing, vision, taste and smell, tactile sensations (including perception of hot and cold) and on proprio-sensitive controls which form the basis of balance, locomotion and manipulation.

Figure 5.1   The Exploratorium is housed in the Palace of Fine Arts on the San Francisco waterfront. (The Exploratorium, San Francisco, USA.)

The location of the new museum was a matter for careful consideration (Hein, 1990, pp. 15–21), and San Francisco was seen as the kind of city that would be responsive to new ideas and new types of cultural institutions. The Exploratorium opened in 1969 in an unusual building on the San Francisco waterfront looking out towards the Golden Gate Bridge. The building had been erected in 1915 for the Panama-Pacific exposition as the Palace of Fine Art; the architect, Bernard Maybeck, had intended this to be a temporary structure, but under pressure the City of San Francisco decided to maintain the building and it was used for a variety of purposes (see Figure 5.1). By the 1960s the structure had to be substantially rebuilt, and the City agreed to allow Oppenheimer to use part of the building rent-free for his Exploratorium project. The Palace of Fine Art became the Palace of Arts and Science and formed a fitting home for a project intended to demonstrate the closeness of art to science.

The Exploratorium houses a vast array of ingenious devices designed to surprise and delight visitors of all ages and all backgrounds. In 1969, the interior of the Palace of Fine Art resembled an aircraft hangar (Exploratorium, 1982, pp. 3–4), and Oppenheimer decided to concentrate on filling the space with exhibits rather than altering the design of the building. The basic nature of the interior finishes and the cavernous structure give the Exploratorium a rough-and-ready feeling. Exhibits, many of which look like bits of laboratory apparatus hastily strung together, provide an introduction to a host of physical phenomena. Oppenheimer followed his exhibit plan based on perception, so there are sections covering touch, taste, light and sound. New exhibits have been devised, and since 1969 many new sections have been added including electricity, animal behaviour, colour, heat and temperature. Oppenheimer and his staff were not concerned to make the exhibits look attractive; rather, they aimed to develop exhibits which would surprise visitors with whatever phenomena were being explored and which would arouse their curiosity and encourage further exploration. Many exhibits are counter-intuitive; for example, in the Gray Step exhibit visitors move a rope that covers the boundary between two seemingly identical white rectangles, whereupon one rectangle looks uniformly dark grey and one looks uniformly white. The effect is startling and completely unexpected and visitors often repeat the procedure, trying to understand the effect. A careful examination of the exhibit reveals that what appeared uniformly white rectangles were really rectangles which get gradually darker across their width. The rope simply hides the discontinuity.

Exhibits covering the same topic are grouped together so that visitors can gain understanding by exploring similar phenomena again and again from slightly different angles (Oppenheimer, 1980). Most exhibits can be used in many different ways and visitors are expected and encouraged to experiment. Comprehensive labelling tells visitors what to do and what they should be able to see, and asks the question, 'So what?' This final section of each text is designed to help visitors link the exhibit with other scientific ideas and to encourage them to think more deeply about what they have just experienced. Like the exhibits themselves, the graphics are very basic, using little illustrative material but relying almost exclusively on text. Visitors also receive help and information from 'explainers' who staff the gallery (Exploratorium, 1982, p. 11; Preuss, 1982). Explainers are generally high school students who work part-time at the Exploratorium for about a four-month period. They have a variety of academic backgrounds and they receive some payment, although not a great deal. Working in museums either on a voluntary or low-paid basis is fairly common in the USA; volunteers gain additional academic training and the satisfaction of contributing to the community, and museums gain a pool of willing and often highly motivated staff.

Oppenheimer's central aim was to help visitors to the Exploratorium to a better understanding of nature (Starr, 1982). He wanted to break down cultural and other barriers which discourage people from investigating the world around them. His central theme of perception enabled him to include the work of artists in his museum. In 1974 the first artist-in-residence joined the Exploratorium and created the Tactile Tree, a structure which provided many different touch sensations (Hein, 1990, pp. 162–9). Since then artists have developed many exhibits which complement other Exploratorium exhibits and provide islands of spectacular beauty (see Figure 5.2). For example, the Sun Painting uses long prisms and narrow mirrors to create colours from sunlight showing an ever-changing example of the dispersion of white light. More recently, musicians have joined the Exploratorium on short residencies to encourage visitors to explore the nature of sound through music.

Figure 5.2   'Vortex', an exhibit by Doug Hollis, an artist working at the
Exploratorium through its Artist in Residence Programme. (The
Exploratorium, San Francisco, USA.)

During its first ten years the Exploratorium spent 7 million dollars on operation and development. Funds came from government agencies, individuals, charitable foundations, visitor entrance fees and income generated by the museum shop. Oppenheimer had extensive experience of securing grants as an academic scientist, and in the early years of the Exploratorium these skills proved extremely valuable. By 1975, the annual operating budget was a little over $3.5 million, a relatively modest sum for a major US attraction. The City of San Francisco continues to support the museum by providing the Palace of Fine Arts and by regular grants. However, compared to many institutions the Exploratorium is not a wealthy organisation. There is little commercial sponsorship in evidence, which is unusual for a cultural institution in the US of the 1980s and 1990s. The Exploratorium seems to cultivate this financial purity, allowing them to pursue their own ideas unencumbered by the pressures of the commercial world. It has meant that exhibits are generally fairly low-tech – few use complicated electronic or computer mechanisms, and none are cased in elaborate housings. This economical approach to exhibit building is one of the reasons why their designs are regularly adopted by other developing organisations.

Frank Oppenheimer died in 1985, but his influence remains strong. The force of his ideas and his commitment to the project explains in part why the Exploratorium has become such an example to professionals elsewhere. From the beginning staff were keen to share their ideas, and in the late 1970s the first *Exploratorium Cookbook* by Ray Bruman was published, giving details of a wide range of successful exhibits (Bruman, 1987.) The second and third *Cookbooks* by Ron Hipschman were published in 1980 and 1987 (Hipschman, 1980, 1987). The *Cookbooks* provide sketches of each exhibit, details of where to purchase parts and equipment, advice on tricky features, and the text for the label used at the Exploratorium. The clear descriptions and honest evaluations have provided the first steps towards hands-on galleries for many museums throughout the world. The generosity of ideas says much for the kind of organisation the Exploratorium has become. The main aim remains the proselytising of science and technology through exhibits, explainers, and by inspiring others to do likewise.

Figure 5.3   The Ontario Science Centre. Its complex of buildings was designed
to fit into the landscape of Toronto's Don Valley. (Ontario Science
Centre, Toronto, Canada.)

The Ontario Science Centre

The Ontario Science Centre opened in 1969 within months of the
Exploratorium. Although each institution presents science in very
different ways, both have become internationally recognised for their
work in encouraging positive attitudes to science and technology,
especially among young people.

The Ontario Science Centre was an ambitious project undertaken
by the provincial government of Ontario as part of the centennial
celebrations of the state of Canada (Ontario Science Centre, 1979).
Initially a museum commemorating Canada's contributions to
science, technology and transport was envisaged. However, as the
plans developed in the committees which brought together museum
professionals, scientists and industrialists, the emphasis shifted from

historical artefacts to exhibits which would demonstrate scientific principles and their applications.

In 1964 the Ontario government commissioned the architect Raymond Moriyama to design a new building in Toronto for the Science Centre (Moriyama *et al.*, 1969). He produced a stunning complex of buildings which provide interesting and varied display areas, with walkways which link the various sections of the Centre looking out across the Don Valley. Construction costs totalled $23 million, much to the despair of the Ontario government who watched the figures spiral from the original estimate of $14 million (see Figure 5.3).

The project proved to be a complex administrative operation. In 1966 William O'Dea, then Senior Keeper of Aeronautics at the London Science Museum, was persuaded to accept the post of Director General. His guidance provided a link between the traditional museum approach of artefact-based displays with the new ideas of hands-on exhibits. He suggested the development of the Science Arcade, an area where children could play games, try quizzes and investigate a wide range of gadgets. His leadership also linked the Centre with the London Science Museum, then the most prestigious institution in the world.

Unlike the Exploratorium, the display style developed at the Ontario Science Centre was not the product of one man's dream. Instead, many different designers and scientists worked together to create exhibits. A number of basic principles were agreed at the outset: visitors should be able to touch as many exhibits as possible, and exhibits should arouse the curiosity of the visitor. The Director of Interpretation Taizo Miake guided this process, translating ideas into workable designs (Moriyama *et al.*, 1969). Although the Centre does not purport to be a historical museum, its displays do incorporate historical artefacts where appropriate. Science is interpreted very broadly here; topics such as costume, food and sport have been included in exhibitions since 1969, demonstrating the science of everyday life. It is a distinction worth noting that, unlike the Exploratorium, the Ontario Science Centre has not set out to explore physical phenomena in any systematic way; rather, it has taken traditional exhibition themes such as transport and developed new interpretative techniques, providing a range of different ways in which the visitor can interact with exhibits (see Figures 5.4, 5.5).

The standard of finish of the exhibits is very high indeed. With

Figure 5.4   'See Yourself Walk', an exhibit in the Sport Area, Ontario Science
Centre. (Ontario Science Centre, Toronto, Canada.)

over a million visitors a year, exhibits need to be robust. Supporting
graphics are professionally presented, providing background information and illustrations to each section of the display. 'Hosts' are
available to explain exhibits further or to help visitors use the
various devices; they also provide a programme of small demonstrations of various kinds at regular intervals throughout the day. For
example, in the electricity exhibition a Van De Graff generator is
demonstrated, making young visitors' hair stand on end. Presentations like this bring the Centre to life, adding a sense of excitement
and a lively human feel to the exhibitions. Hosts are usually college
students trained in science and presentation techniques by the
Centre.

The Ontario Science Centre is a success story for the province.
The provincial government reward this success with generous
funding; in 1988/9 the Centre received over $12 million of provincial

Figure 5.5 'Action/Reaction' in the Science Arcade, Ontario Science Centre. (Ontario Science Centre, Toronto, Canada.)

funds (Ontario Science Centre, 1989). In addition, commercial sponsors provide considerable sums towards the capital costs of new exhibitions. Such funding makes possible a large staff including exhibit developers, designers, workshop craftsmen and technicians.

Since 1973, travelling exhibitions have taken the Centre to communities in distant parts of the province. The success of the 'Science Circus' has been outstanding (Ontario Science Centre, 1979). The Centre has also sent exhibits to Australia, Mexico, the United Kingdom and Saudia Arabia. These temporary exhibitions have often been the starting point for the development of permanent science centres around the world.

North American science centres

Neither the Exploratorium nor the Ontario Science Centre invented hands-on exhibits. As mentioned above in Chapter 3, Jean Perrin's Palais de la Découverte which opened in Paris in 1937 was based largely on demonstrations and interactive exhibits. However, there can be no doubt that the participatory style taken up and developed by the Exploratorium and the Ontario Science Centre shaped the development of both established institutions and new projects throughout North America during the following decade. In 1973, the Association of Science and Technology Centers was formed, providing a formal vehicle for the exchange of ideas and information. This exchange takes place through ASTC's regular newsletters and other publications, and through its conferences – major events in the calendar of North American science museums.

A glance through the ASTC's guide to contemporary science and technology museums demonstrates the number and range of such institutions across the continent (Association of Science and Technology Centers, 1980). Many, like the Franklin Institute's science museum in Philadelphia and the Chicago Museum of Science and Industry are long established. Both opened to the public in 1933 as museums demonstrating, through exhibitions of industrial and scientific artefacts, the story of science and technology. The history of the Chicago Museum has already been described in some detail. Here we should note the increasing commitment to a hands-on approach since the 1970s. Victor Danilov, Director from 1971 until 1985, was particularly keen to emphasise the role of the museum as a public educator (Museum of Science and Industry, 1983, p. 25). Similarly, over the past twenty years the Franklin Institute's displays have incorporated hands-on exhibits in increasing numbers. Although the Institute continues to display its historic exhibits, including an impressive collection of patent models, it has increasingly become a place where 'doing' is more important than just 'looking'. Again, the Boston Science Museum, which originated from the city's Society of Natural History founded in 1830, now displays few specimens of flora or fauna, and exhibits concentrate instead on contemporary topics. Following Ontario's lead, the museum has developed a range of short presentations which occur at regular intervals throughout the day.

Many other science museums in both the US and Canada are of

more recent origin. Some, like the Maryland Science Center in Baltimore, openly express their indebtedness to the Exploratorium. Their 'Science Arcade', a title borrowed from Ontario, uses recipes from the *Cookbook* to create a series of exhibits exploring optical, magnetic and other physical phenomena. Others have incorporated the style more subtly, using the hands-on approach as a design principle. The California Museum of Science and Industry has, like Chicago, secured sponsorship from industry for many of its exhibits. Exhibitions here are very high-tech, using the most modern electronic and computer control techniques available and a highly stylised format.

Although not established as science museums, children's museums have both contributed to and benefited from this spread of participatory science centres. Two museums in the US stand out as worthy of note. The first is the long-established Brooklyn Children's Museum in New York, and the second is the Boston Children's Museum whose educational programmes have helped proselytise interactive museums (Montagu, 1984). The Brooklyn Museum encourages children to learn by studying objects. Demonstrations are given introducing children to small animals, for example, and other objects are used from the museum's collections, including dolls and ethnographic materials such as clothing. The Boston Museum encourages activities among its visitors by allowing them, for example, to become television news presenters for a few moments and providing a range of interactive exhibits themed under topics such as 'water'. Both could be described as science museums for the very young.

Science centres in North America have proved highly successful institutions. They have attracted large audiences who return time and time again. They have received large sums of sponsorship money which have enabled a wide range of different types of exhibits to be developed. Their educational potential has been recognised and exploited, through classes provided for school children both as part of the school curriculum and as more informal programmes developed as holiday activities. These links between school and museum are very strong in many parts of North America partly because of its geographical size. Most children in the UK are able to get to London for a day and a visit to the Science Museum is therefore possible. In the US, San Francisco may be a four-hour plane journey away. The local science centre therefore constitutes an important resource for teachers.

The final element in the success of these institutions, apart from the talent of the exhibit developers, is the tradition in North America of volunteering. This has provided museums of all different types with a pool of enthusiastic free labour. Along with the high school and college students who are also available at very little cost, these individuals provide links with the community as well as valuable adjuncts to full-time permanent staff.

The UK follows suit

It is somewhat ironic that although many of the ideas for both the Exploratorium and the Ontario Science Centre came from Britain, interactive science exhibitions did not appear here until the 1980s. The circle was then completed with the two North American pioneers providing inspiration and assistance to a number of projects around Britain.

The Exploratory, as its name suggests, is very similar in style to the Exploratorium. Its founder, Professor Richard Gregory, is a psychologist of international reputation whose writings on visual perception have become well known. As well as an interest in perception, Gregory and Oppenheimer also shared an interest in philosophy. They met soon after the Exploratorium opened and Gregory was able to suggest ideas for exhibits which extended the theme of visual perception (Gregory, 1987). They became friends and correspondents, and Oppenheimer gave much encouragement to Gregory's plans for a science centre in Britain.

During the 1970s, Gregory became involved in a number of exhibitions concerning perception. The first, at the Institute of Contemporary Arts, was prepared in association with the Institute's Director, Sir Roger Penrose and the art historian, Sir Ernst Gombrich. This project was eventually published as a book, *Illusion in Nature and Art*, edited by Gregory and Gombrich. This project was assisted by Sheila Grinell of the Exploratorium who was lent by Oppenheimer for six months. Sheila Grinell later headed the Association of Science and Technology Centers in the US and subsequently, the New York Hall of Science.

The second project was a section of the Human Biology gallery at the Natural History Museum. The museum's pioneering head of interpretation, Roger Miles, asked Gregory to help with the design and later the re-design of the section on perception. This gallery broke new ground for science exhibitions in the UK, being concept-based rather than object-based. It has proved hugely successful in its provocative approach, challenging visitors to explore and question a range of issues relating to the way we see ourselves.

Gregory was much encouraged by the success of this project and by the late 1970s had decided to seek the necessary advice and support to set up a hands-on science centre along the lines of the San Francisco Exploratorium. A small grant from the Nuffield Foundation allowed Gregory and his associates, including Priscilla Heard, a lecturer in Gregory's Department of Psychology at Bristol University, to arrange a number of initial meetings. By 1982, Bristol had been decided upon as the Exploratory's home and a trustee committee including prominent local people had been organised. The Exploratory is now a company limited by guarantee with charitable status.

Further grants from the Nuffield Foundation provided sufficient money to set up a workshop, and £20,000 from one of the Sainsbury family trusts funded a temporary exhibition at the annual meeting of the British Association for the Advancement of Science, an event guaranteed to provide publicity in the national press and in the specialist scientific journals. This, and a further temporary exhibition in January 1985, convinced the Nuffield Foundation of the project's viability, and major grants of £120,000 and £130,000 followed. This was the essential boost the project required, and it became possible to appoint workshop staff and look for a permanent home. Initially the Exploratory opened in the Victoria Rooms, an elegant neo-classical building in Clifton. In 1988, the project moved to the restored Bristol Old Station, Temple Meads, whose cavernous interior provides room for workshops and display areas.

Like the Exploratorium, exhibits at the Exploratory tend to have a raw feel to them. In part, the lack of design finish serves to make them less intimidating, particularly to children and to adults with little scientific background. Gregory and his colleagues aimed to create a place where exploring the universe through science could be fun, interesting and rewarding. The themes taken up at the museum began with Gregory's passion for perception, and in particular, visual puns. There are also sections on light and colour, while exhibits demonstrating principles of technology provide a more wide-ranging introduction to science (Glancy (ed.), 1980) (see Figure 5.6).

Figure 5.6   The main floor of the Exploratory makes full use of the space
provided at the former Bristol Temple Meads Station. (Martin
Haswell: The Exploratory, Bristol.)

Despite a number of substantial grants from several of the best
known educational charities in the UK including the Carnegie Trust
and the Fairburn Trust, the Exploratory continues to struggle to
make ends meet. Visitor entrance fees provide running costs, but
the capital needs of projects such as these are such that independent
organisations continue to struggle.

In contrast to the 'string-and-sealing-wax' development of the
Exploratory, the London Science Museum began in the mid-1980s
to set up a new, hugely expensive gallery based entirely on interactive exhibits (Wilson, 1987). The Science Museum was originally
intended as an inspiration to both students and those involved in
developing new technologies. The Children's Gallery, an initiative
of the 1930s, was designed to arouse the curiosity of visitors while
demonstrating the principles of science. These overtly educational

rather than antiquarian aims were echoed in the mid-1970s when space in a building close to the Science Museum in central London was made available as possible exhibition space. A 'Hall of Experiments' was planned to contrast and complement the historical displays at South Kensington. In the event the space was allocated for storage and the ideas for interactive exhibits had to be put on hold. However, the Ontario Science Circus visited the London Science Museum in 1981. Public response was very positive, and this enthusiasm strengthened suggestions put forward by the education service of the museum, headed by Anthony Wilson, for an exhibition area permanently devoted to similar hands-on exhibits. Early in 1984, with funding from the Department of Trade and Industry and the Leverhulme Trust, Dame Margaret Weston, the museum's Director, announced that Launch Pad, a major new interactive gallery, would open within three years. During the development phase for Launch Pad there would be a number of Test Beds – temporary exhibitions which would allow the project team to test out prototype exhibits on visitors over a period of about six weeks.

Launch Pad grew out of ideas from the education service of the museum. While members of this department played an important role in the development of the finished gallery, a large team, including curators seconded from other departments and new members of staff, was assembled. The process of developing exhibits was refined into a series of phases involving different combinations of individuals at different stages. From the outside, the process, involving numerous production meetings, appeared bureaucratic to say the least, but it worked and Launch Pad opened in July 1986 with sixty-five exhibits covering 900 square metres.

The Science Museum is one of London's busiest visitor attractions, with about 1.5 million visitors each year. Because of the large numbers of people, any interactive exhibits had to be extremely robust. The museum's designers decided to use kee-klamp as the standard structural framework for exhibits. In the prototype stage this gave the Test Bed exhibits a feeling of sturdiness, while in final exhibits the scaffolding-type frame was modified somewhat to give a more polished finish.

The large numbers of visitors to the museum posed problems because too many people in the gallery at any one time is both dangerous and unpleasant. A system of 'time-ticketing' was

Figure 5.7   'Hosts' helping young visitors explore the effects of air pressure in
Launch Pad, Science Museum, London. (Science Museum, London.)

therefore introduced: visitors could collect tickets for Launch Pad
when they arrived at the museum. This ticket gives a time when
they are allowed admission. Generally this system is preferable to
those where visitors are given an end-time, as it is unpleasant and
extremely difficult to throw visitors out of a gallery, whereas it is
quite acceptable to refuse them entry for a short while. Most visitors
tended to stay for about an hour to an hour and a half so that it
proved feasible to regulate numbers fairly accurately.

Launch Pad is a noisy, busy place. Exhibits covering similar
topics are grouped together, but there is no overall strong theme.
The emphasis tends towards technology rather than purely physical
phenomena; many of the exhibits demonstrate how certain machines
work (Wilson, Watt and Quin, 1988). For example, one display
allows visitors to discover how rolling bearings are constructed and
why they are used so extensively in machines. Other exhibits show

the principles of structures: visitors can try their skills at making an arch bridge and walking over it. Surprisingly perhaps, the graphics on the exhibits do not make strong links to historical exhibits in other parts of the museum, although these links are highlighted in the colour guide published to accompany the exhibition. Short instructions are given on each exhibit. Further information is given on 'bats' hanging from the sides of the display, and there are also 'information points' where files containing articles and other details about each topic in the gallery are kept. The gallery is staffed by 'hosts', who tend to be young people on temporary contracts. Training is provided by members of the museum education service (see Figure 5.7).

Launch Pad's predecessor, the Children's Gallery, has been largely displaced in its role as the museum's principal activity for children. In consequence it is soon to be disbanded and merged with its large and more vigorous successor. Launch Pad is intended to become the focus for the Science Museum's education service, providing an expanded service for schools and teachers. It was an expensive project to set up – £1 million was spent before it even opened (Wilson, 1987, pp. 39–40) – but it has proved popular among Science Museum visitors, and it has provided a showcase for hands-on science in the UK, a source of both ideas and advice for other fledgling projects.

When Dame Margaret Weston announced plans for the development of Launch Pad she was also able to announce the setting up of a fund by the Gatsby Trust, a charity of the Sainsbury family, to provide seed-capital grants for smaller projects outside London. Professor John Beetlestone, then Professor of Science Education at University College Cardiff, heard this news when attending a lecture given by Dame Margaret at the Royal Society of Arts in the summer of 1984 (Beetlestone, 1987). Since taking up his post in Cardiff in 1977 he had been involved in projects designed to arouse people's interest in science and technology, such as Science Week where theatrical presentations using a science or technology theme are put on at the Sherman Theatre, Cardiff. Beetlestone saw the Gatsby grants as the means to bring an interactive science centre into being for Wales. With the support of Dr Bill Bevan, Principal of University College, Cardiff, and Dr Douglas Bassett, Director of the National Museum of Wales, he brought together a group of people to suggest exhibit ideas and to develop a formal structure for the project. From this group of people he also set up a 'finance and management group' involving members of the local commercial community. In November 1985, Wales Gas offered the first floor of their showrooms in the pedestrian shopping precinct in Cardiff free of charge for November/December 1986. Gatsby agreed to fund the building of exhibits for this temporary exhibition, which was by then seen as the first phase towards setting up a permanent science centre. Ken Gleason, formerly of the Museum of Science Discovery in Harrisburg, Pennsylvania was recruited as exhibits director, and he took charge of building exhibits for the temporary exhibition in July 1986. Techniquest, as the project was now called, opened after a very short time with forty-eight exhibits in an area of 666 square metres on 13 November 1986. In 1989 Techniquest moved into larger, permanent accomodation. Staff continue to experiment with new exhibit ideas, and in 1991 Chemiquest, a project designed to encourage exhibits which provide opportunities for exploring aspects of chemistry, was launched.

Another project given substance by the Gatsby grants was Technology Testbed by the National Museums on Merseyside at their large object store (Sudbury, 1987). The exhibition of about twenty interactive exhibits helped liven up the store which was already opened to the public on a regular basis. The exhibits were intended to help visitors, especially children, understand something of the technology on display. Some were largely undesigned, and presentation was fairly crude to say the least. However, Testbed was undoubtedly popular, proving yet again the demand for hands-on displays. Sadly, Technology Testbed did not survive when the lease for the museum's large object store expired. Nevertheless, the exhibition demonstrated the appeal to visitors of active participation and informed the developments of exhibits elsewhere in the museum.

Elsewhere in the North West, hands-on science became, in the 1980s and 1990s a permanent feature of other museums. In Manchester, the first phase of the Greater Manchester Museum of Science and Industry opened in 1983 in the complex of buildings which had formed the world's first passenger railway station. There was tremendous scope for developing new ways to tell the story of science in Manchester and staff were given encouragement to think as broadly as possible about how and what to communicate to visitors.

When Dame Margaret Weston announced the Science Museum's Launch Pad project, Manchester seemed an obvious location for a similar venture. The museum decided to create a centre which would be Mancunian in feel. As we have already seen above, the city has a long tradition of scientific excellence dating back to the achievements of John Dalton, James Prescott Joule and others. The subject areas suggested by the history of Manchester science were seen as forming the basis for the development of interactive exhibits which would enable visitors to understand better some aspects of what these historical figures were investigating. Although the idea of linking historical displays with hands-on exhibits did not, in fact, come about, the idea of using themes found in other parts of the museum did form an important organising principle for the hands-on gallery when it eventually opened.

Fundraising for the project proved somewhat difficult initially. In part, at least, this was because there was nowhere to house an interactive gallery. Although the site had great potential, the warehouses required major rebuilding to provide suitable exhibition space, and all the other possible sites were already committed for particular exhibitions. The breakthrough which made the whole project possible came with the abolition of the museum's funding authority, the Greater Manchester Council. A large capital sum was made available specifically to renovate the Lower Byrom Street Warehouse and thus provide exhibition space for an interactive science centre. The architects Building Design Partnership were appointed, and planning for how the hands-on display would be developed began.

Many Manchester investigators had been interested in the problems of energy and power. The museum collections include the apparatus of James Prescott Joule, and a gallery exploring the development of electricity generation and transmission had opened in March 1986; energy was therefore one obvious theme for a section of the gallery. The museum also had a number of fine historic microscopes which were already on display and an extensive camera collection; light was an appropriate second theme, allowing us to introduce visitors to some of the phenomena which were exploited in the technology of the instruments which they could see elsewhere in the museum.

Funding for a team of exhibit builders was secured through what was then the Manpower Services Commission, and a project coordinator, Ian Russell, started work in April 1987 and the exhibit builders joined a month later. The first task was to equip a small workshop and to get the team started on some fairly straightforward exhibits. Ideas were borrowed from the Exploratorium, from Launch Pad and from colleagues in science education. The exhibit builders grasped what was needed very quickly and became totally absorbed in the project. Designs for each exhibit evolved as they were being made, with the exhibit builders making important contributions to what became a team effort. Erecto, rectangular steel tubing finished in black, was one of the main construction materials and was used wherever a rigid framework was required. Most of the exhibits were constructed from good quality birch plywood and then painted. John Williams, the museum's Design Officer, suggested a colour scheme reminiscent of a Mondrian painting: mostly grey with patches of brilliant colours emphasised by the black Erecto framework.

One of the most difficult tasks in developing any new exhibition is to think of a name. The project was managed through a working group bringing together staff from different sections of the museum who were involved in one way or another with the science centre. This group brainstormed to find a name and eventually Ian Russell's suggestion of Xperiment! was decided upon. During school holidays groups of exhibits were arranged in temporary displays to enable staff to see visitors using them. The exercise was extremely valuable, not only for discovering design faults, but also for boosting the morale of the exhibit builders who enjoyed seeing the exhibits in use.

As in many other centres, gallery staff were available on Xperiment! to help visitors use the exhibits, but in this case the gallery staff were also the exhibit builders. This has worked extremely well in Manchester because of the commitment of these staff to the project as a whole. They wanted to help people to get the best out of the exhibits they had built, and they also wanted to make sure that the gallery survived the school groups, whose behaviour could both disrupt the enjoyment of others and pose a threat to the exhibits. With one exception, the exhibit builders were not highly educated in science; this proved an advantage because they shared the fresh eyes of many of our visitors. Several training sessions in the principles behind the exhibits were organised to give the exhibit builders confidence and make sure that information given out on the

Figure 5.8 Generating electricity in Xperiment!, the Museum of Science and Industry's hands-on science centre. (Museum of Science and Industry in Manchester.)

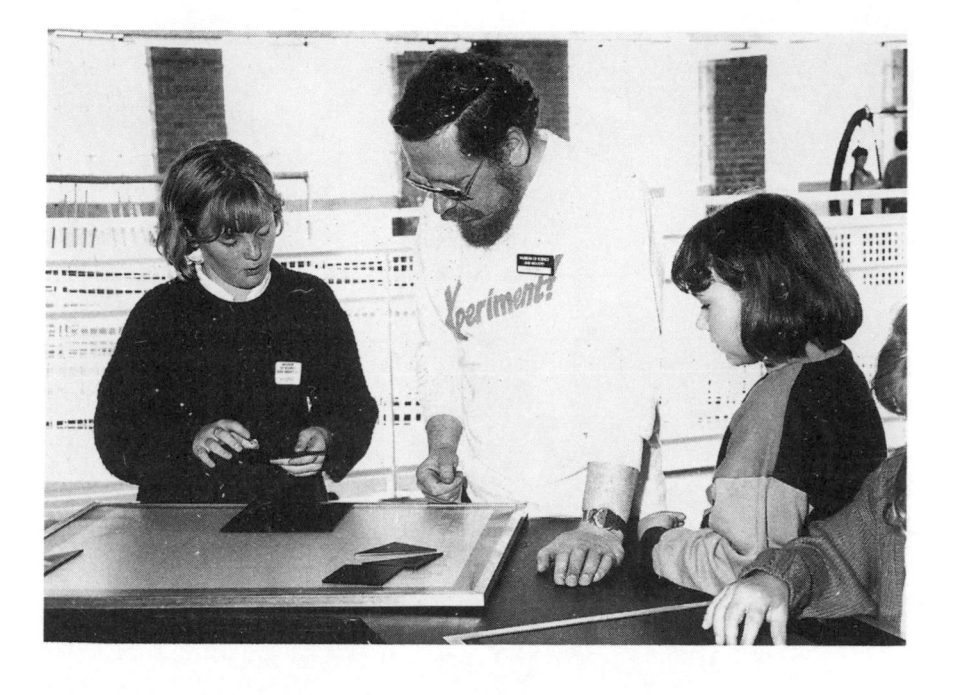

Figure 5.9 One of Xperiment!'s exhibit builders giving some advice on the gallery. (Museum of Science and Industry in Manchester.)

gallery would complement teaching in schools (see Figures 5.8, 5.9).

Funds for exhibits were secured from a number of sources: the City Action Team, a joint initiative between the Department of the Environment and the Department of Trade and Industry, provided £35,000; British Nuclear Fuels Limited gave £10,000; Norweb gave £10,000, the Greater Manchester Youth Association gave £4,000. The Gatsby Trust awarded the project £5,125 to develop strategies for conveying information about the exhibits on the gallery. This money enabled several information sheets about light and energy to be produced and made available to teachers free of charge.

For several years, the museum had offered a Saturday Science Club where children aged from about 7 to 14 years carried out their own investigations and gained British Association for the Advancement of Science (BAAS) medals. The BAAS shares many of the aims of science centres in its concern to widen public awareness of science and technology and promote science to young people through informal out-of-school activities. BAYSDAY, a carnival-like event where young people could try their hands at competitions and hear lectures and debates about topical issues, had become the highspot of the BAAS programme for young people, attracting to its London venue several thousands of visitors. Manchester and Xperiment! seemed an obvious focus for a northern version of this event. A grant from the DTI provided modest funds for expenses; volunteers joined the organising committee, and celebrities such as the television personality, Johnny Ball, agreed to give several presentations and present prizes for the various competitions.

BAYSDAY provided an appropriate celebration of the opening of Xperiment! and provided a marketing vehicle for the new gallery. Each notice of the event, which was mailed to schools and teachers throughout the North West of England, announced the opening of this new hands-on science centre. BAYSDAY and events like them illustrate how hands-on galleries can extend the scope of museums, enabling them to participate in projects with other educational organisations.

A second project to introduce Xperiment! to as wide an audience as possible again involved the BAAS, this time in partnership with the *Daily Telegraph*. Children and adults were asked to try their hands at devising exhibits for the new gallery. The winning entries were offered cash prizes and the chance to see their idea made into an exhibit. Posters were mailed direct to schools, and articles appeared in the science and technology section of the newspaper. The entries were judges by Dr Roger Highfield, technology correspondent on the *Daily Telegraph*, Sir Walter Bodmer, then President of the BAAS and Dr Patrick Greene, Director of the museum. The *Daily Telegraph* funded the construction of the winning exhibit, Optical Snooker, which was a combination of two similar suggestions, one from the adult section and one from the children's section. Both explored how beams of light could be directed by mirrors.

Xperiment! opened in November 1988 and quickly became one of the most popular galleries of the museum, especially with younger visitors. BAYSDAY has become a regular feature of the events programme for both the museum and the BAAS, which now uses an office in the Museum of Science and Industry as its base in the North West. Xperiment! has continued to take themes for new exhibits from the subjects of historical displays elsewhere in the museum, for example, visitors can now explore some of the properties of gases in Xperiment!, while the Gas Gallery provides complementary displays explaining the history of the fuel.

Just as hands-on exhibits in science museums in the US and Canada became vogue in the 1970s, so interactive exhibits are to be seen in numerous museums around the UK in the 1990s. The National Museum of Photography, Film and Television in Bradford features many interactive exhibits throughout its galleries. Hampshire Education Authority have set up a technology centre for teachers and pupils to use in a variety of ways. There is also an itinerant science centre, The Discovery Dome, organised by Steve Pizzey, a veteran of the London Science Museum, the Bristol Exploratory, and the Gatsby Trust which took its distinctive geodesic tents to many towns in Britain in the late 1980s.

There can be little doubt that hands-on displays have made museums more lively places to visit and have increased their appeal for children and young people. Unlike the US, the UK has no tradition of children's museums. There are several museums *of* childhood, but no museums specifically aimed at an audience of children. This absence is soon to be filled by a new institution being developed in Halifax, Yorkshire, to be called Eureka! Although not intended as a science museum, Eureka! will certainly provide an introduction for the very young to the science and technology of everyday life.

The rest of the world

The development of hands-on exhibits during the 1980s was going on, not only in the UK, but throughout the world. In Paris, as noted above, the French government began developing a city-garden complex to provide a combination of leisure and educational facilities. The La Villette complex opened in stages from 1985 and provides Planetarium – exhibitions about science and industry, together with hands-on displays for very young children. In Eindhoven, Holland, the Philips electronics company set up the Evoluon, a science centre based upon exhibits which used the company's products (Schouten, 1966). The Evoluon building resembled a martian space module suspended on the suburban skyline. Sadly, the cost of maintaining the high-tech exhibits proved too onerous for Philips when the recession of the late eighties began to take its toll, and the Evoluon was closed down. In 1984, the City

Figure 5.10 The Powerhouse, Sydney, where hands-on exhibits have been developed alongside historic displays. (Andrew Frolows: Courtesy of the Trustees, Museum of Applied Arts and Sciences, Sydney, Australia.)

of Zurich provided support for a temporary exhibition of interactive science displays. Phaenomena was an impressively ambitious project with both open-air exhibits and smaller displays under cover (Mueller, 1987). After its success in attracting numerous visitors to Zurich's major parks, Phaenomena toured several other cities. In other European cities, museums have adapted their styles of display incorporating the hands-on approach. The organisation ECSITE, with offices in Helsinki, now provides communications between these European centres, with newsletters, workshops and other meetings.

In Australia, the New South Wales Museum of Applied Arts and Science, which dated back to an international exhibition in 1879, re-opened in 1988 as the Powerhouse Museum, combining hands-on displays (such as the Kids interactive discovery spaces aimed at visitors under 8 years of age) with exhibitions showing some of the

Figure 5.11   Questacon is now housed in magnificent new buildings in
Canberra. (Questacon, The National Science and Technology
Centre, Canberra, Australia.)

museum's valuable historical collections (O'Brien and Donaldson,
1989) (see Figure 5.10). Powerhouse's opening was scheduled to
commemorate Australia's bicentenary (Greene, 1989). In Canberra,
Questacon, a new interactive science centre, provided another
bicentennial project. Questacon had opened in 1980 with about
fifteen exhibits devised by Michael Gore, a physicist at the
Australian National University. It was soon attracting a large
audience, and in 1985 a science centre using Questacon as its model
was adopted as a national bicentennial project (National Science and
Technology Centre, 1989). Japan became a partner in the project,
contributing over 500 million yen to the building cost. Australia's
National Science and Technology Centre opened in 1988, providing
an impressive demonstration of the popularity of hands-on science.
In less than nine months from the opening of its doors, the Centre

Figure 5.12 Questacon's version of an exhibit exploring air pressure.
(Questacon, The National Science and Technology Centre,
Canberra, Australia.)

attracted more than 365,000 visitors (see Figures 5.11, 5.12).

Hands-on science centres are sometimes seen as catalysts for the development of science education in the surrounding area. This was the aim behind the setting up of Science North in Sudbury by the Ontario provincial government. It was also the aim behind many of the science centres which have been set up in India recently. Science, as we know it, is part of western culture, often quite strange to those who have been brought up with different ways of understanding the world. The government of India hope that the many science centres being established there can help make science and technology, essential to the country's modernisation, more accessible. The size of the country means that it is important to develop a network of such institutions so that their facilities can become as widely available as possible.

Conclusions

During the 1980s in the UK there was considerable interest in and concern about the lack of science understanding among the public at large. Projects were set up to improve 'scientific literacy' among both adults and children. The development of interactive science centres was part of this movement, gaining momentum from other projects such as the BAAS initiatives. How effective science centres prove in this aim will probably not be known until long-term research projects into their influence become available. In any case their influence on individuals is probably impossible to record in any comprehensive statistical sense. However, many observations confirm that these types of exhibitions do change people's perceptions of what science means. They make people realise that science does not just go on in laboratories where clever people carry out complicated experiments, but is about understanding and exploring the world; you don't have to be a genius to be able to do that.

Since the 1970s, science centres have also contributed to a changing perception of museums among the public. In North America the term 'museum' has long had a wider meaning than in the UK, with less emphasis on object collections. The Ontario Science Centre and the Exploratorium has placed very little emphasis on objects, using them sparingly, if at all. Science museums have become museums of concepts, rather than museums devoted to preserving the past.

As we have seen from the experience of the Ontario Science Centre and the Launch Pad project in London, interactive exhibitions can be enormously expensive to set up. When open, they need a wide range of resources to ensure that visitors do not meet too many 'exhibit out of action' signs. They also need resources to ensure continuing innovation; a hands-on gallery where nothing new has been added for a couple of years usually appears lifeless and in need of care and attention. At the London Science Museum, I suspect that a scaling-down of Launch Pad during the 1990s will take place as workshop and other staff resources are needed elsewhere. It will be interesting to see how other centres evolve and change during the next decade, particularly those which have been set up as independent charitable organisations. For them the problem of resources is always immediate, especially where finances are crucially dependent on visitor income.

Many science centres have been set up as overtly educational ventures. For example, the Hampshire Technology Centre is funded in part by the Local Education Authority. Hands-on centres have strengthened the links between museums and schools, providing resources which are seen by teachers as directly relevant to the classroom. In the UK, the introduction of a national curriculum has accelerated the introduction of science teaching in primary schools teaching 5–11-year-olds. Science museums with hands-on resources provide both teachers and pupils with ideas and materials which they can take back to their classrooms and develop there. Many museums, including the Science and Industry Museum in Manchester, have organised special programmes involving the children in setting up discovery centres for themselves back at school. These grass-roots links are valuable to museums not only for their strictly educational merit, but because they provide a channel of communication to sectors of the community not often reached by conventional marketing techniques, which generally includes those groups not usually regarded as typical museum visitors.

My final observation concerns circles which may or may not be ever decreasing. Kenneth Hudson has observed that the science centres of today demonstrating the marvels of the most up-to-date technology fast become the museums of tomorrow (Hudson, 1987, p. 112). This has happened with the Science Museum in London, with the Deutsches Museum in Munich and what is now the Power House in Sydney. All began as institutions celebrating contemporary achievements in science and technology; all became antiquarian museums documenting the history of those achievements. Each has subsequently regained something of the celebratory function through interactive displays. Such exhibits have brought museums back to their original aims of public enlightenment in the broadest possible sense. Whether the cycle will continue to turn, only time will tell.

6. *Frameworks of knowledge*

Science and technology are not easy subjects to portray through museums. Science is essentially concept-based, a knowledge system about the natural world; objects from science museum collections are often understandable only in terms of the ideas they helped form or served to uphold. Technology lends itself more easily to display, but often the vital innovation within the machine on view is not apparent. Nevertheless, despite these problems, museums offering visitors glimpses of science and technology have become popular attractions throughout the world.

Most of the major science museums in the world were set up to educate the public about the nature and content of science and technology. The educational aims of, for example, the Science Museum in London, the Deutsches Museum in Munich or the Centre for Science and Industry at La Villette in Paris have set these science and technology museums apart from those institutions founded to care for and preserve other aspects of our cultural heritage. Within art museums devoted to anthropology or archeology, emphasis is generally upon the academic study of the collection. In some senses science museums have always been more visitor-orientated, less precious and ultimately, in aim if not in content, concerned about the future. Young visitors are seen as potential practitioners, encouraged by displays which capture their imagination. But practitioners of what? What do we mean when we talk about science? Science has become institutionalised since the second half of the nineteenth century, providing academic and industrial careers for those trained in its disciplines. Science is now a highly regarded form of knowledge. 'Scientific' reports are afforded much status. What, then, sets science apart from other kinds of knowledge such as astrology or 'common sense'? How can museums convey the special nature of this knowledge through the artefacts of those who generate its ideas?

The framework of knowledge

At the beginning of this book we noted that science is a knowledge system which attempts to make sense of the physical world by suggesting theories which explain observations and experiments. How do these theories come about? By what criteria are theories evaluated? Science today is largely self-regulated; scientists decide which theories are valid according to the methods and procedures adopted. Ideas have changed over time, and we must consider the circumstances in which scientists reject accepted ideas and adopt new interpretations of physical phenomena. There is a vast literature exploring these very difficult questions which involve the philosophy and sociology of science. Different models have been suggested for the ways in which scientists operate (Losee, 1980). It would be inappropriate here to try to survey this subject in depth, but it is important that we examine the cognitive nature of scientific knowledge and consider the implications for the presentation both of contemporary science and the history of science in museums.

First of all let us consider the procedures through which theories are generated. These procedures are often referred to as 'scientific method'. Appropriate methods are regarded as essential in producing knowledge which can be regarded as 'scientific' – that is, valid interpretations of the world based on 'facts'. One of the most influential writers of this century, the philosopher Karl Popper, focused on the importance of empirical methodology in the formation of scientific thought (Popper, 1972a; Magee, 1975). For Popper, scientific theories are based on empirical evidence – results of experiments and carefully recorded information. Theories are generalised statements which attempt to explain the relationships between various sets of empirical data. They allow scientists to predict what should happen, as well as explain what has been observed. A scientific theory must be testable. Popper proposed that theories should be structured so that they might be constantly exposed to falsification; scientists should structure their investigations, not to seek confirmation of the theory in question, but to search for experiments which will disprove the theory. For example, if we believe that water freezes at 0 degrees centigrade, we can test that theory by searching for instances which confirm this theory. However, we cannot be certain that water will always freeze at 0 degrees centigrade: a better test would be to design experiments to see if there are circumstances when water freezes at a different temperature – we would perhaps investigate the effects of adding salt to water, or observing whether water freezes at 0 degrees at high altitudes. By designing investigations to refute the original theory, we should accumulate enough information to suggest that, in its current form, the theory is inadequate. The empirical evidence for the refutation should form the basis for revising the theory to take account of inconsistent observations. The revised theory should, of course, be as refutable as the original. In such a manner, Popper asserts, knowledge has progressed, one theory giving way to another as it is falsified by judicious experiment carried out by disinterested scientists in pursuit of truth (Popper, 1972b).

A very different view of the way scientists operate has been presented by the historian Thomas Kuhn in his celebrated volume, *The Structure of Scientific Revolutions* (Kuhn, 1962). Kuhn presents us with suggestions of how scientific change has occurred by looking at the reaction of practitioners to experimental results which disagree with the theories they uphold and by examining how scientists structure their investigations.

Kuhn distinguished two modes in which science has tended to operate historically. These he named 'normal science' and 'revolutionary science'. 'Normal science' refers to science practised by most practitioners on a day-to-day basis. It involves working within a 'paradigm', that is, a framework of knowledge which a group of practitioners is using at that time in history. The paradigm is not a single theory, but rather a knowledge system outlined in textbooks, promulgated by lectures and taught through laboratory exercises. Its framework provides ideas for the individual investigations scientists will undertake and the means of solving them. Thus, normal science takes the form of what Kuhn calls 'puzzle-solving'. The paradigm provides a set of rules by which experiments can be designed and their results interpreted. Investigators may undertake to determine a better value for a universal constant or to investigate situations not elaborated initially by the paradigm. This framework also forms the basis through which trainee scientists can be initiated into the discipline.

Science proceeds undisturbed so long as the application of the paradigm continues to explain the phenomena observed. Kuhn suggests that where there is strong commitment to the paradigm, anomalies will generally be explained away as experimental error or special cases.

Revolutionary science is essentially the replacement of one paradigm with another. Kuhn argues that this kind of change is not brought about by one or two anomalous observations. He also suggests that practitioners are not simply falsifying theories as in the Popperian model of science. Revolutions in scientific thought occur when alternative paradigms become available. Alternative paradigms may be developed as responses to persistent anomalies accumulated as part of the practice of normal science within the pre-existing paradigm. Such anomalies give rise to crisis within the community. The victorious paradigm will deal with the anomalies in a constructive way, producing a complete reinterpretation or *gestalt* shift of the research world. The new paradigm will not only provide the means to explain the anomalies which gave rise to the crisis of the old paradigm, but will suggest new problems to explore, new kinds of instruments and new ways of interpreting old data. Although the new paradigm may incorporate something of the old, the rules of the game will have changed, making the two systems incompatible.

Kuhn based his ideas on interpretations of major shifts in scientific thought, such as the emergence of Copernican astronomy or the acceptance of Lavoisier's oxygen theory of combustion. His work has been much debated, many objecting to the imposition of a model of change on historical development. Nevertheless, his ideas have stimulated productive debate about the cognitive nature of science and how that cognitive structure forms the basis for a social system of active practitioners. His ideas lie at the heart of much modern sociology of science which stresses the relationship between knowledge systems and their social context.

We generally assume that scientific knowledge is based on facts, that is, observations and data derived from experiments upon which we can rely. This implies some kind of certainty – perhaps truth. However, scientists make observations and collect measurements from experiments which, according to a Kuhnian model of science, are designed according to a predetermined set of rules and from which a particular result is expected. The instruments used will be those appropriate to the framework of ideas within which the investigator is working. A different set of ideas will necessitate different apparatus because a different set of measurements will be required. At the level of sensory perception, the investigator will see what the paradigm or theory leads him or her to expect (Gombrich, 1962, pp. 53–173). This is not a matter of deliberate bias or lack of judgement on the part of scientists, but an inevitable part of human experience. Experiments in psychology indicate that people 'see' different effects even with identical images on their retinas. Similarly, two people receiving the same impression on their retinas can interpret them as completely different images. 'Facts' cannot be separated from the experiences and the previous knowledge of people gathering them. The inevitable subjectivity of observations and experimental data is still relevant to the Popperian model of scientific progress; structuring investigations to falsify a premise implies an expectation of the results, and such expectations will help form the perceptions of the investigator. Scientific truth, it seems, cannot be absolute.

Museums of science and technology have generally come into being to promote a certain status for science. In the UK, the development of the London Science Museum can be seen as part of the process through which scientists sought recognition as professionals, producing useful and authoritative knowledge. It is not surprising, then, that science is presented by museums as certain knowledge, arrived at through painstaking, objective research. The past is more often than not depicted as a prelude to our present knowledge which, it is hoped, will provide a springboard to future advances. Yet, as we have seen, if we analyse how science actually works, it is impossible to separate observations or 'facts' from theories; each are dependent on the other. Our scientific knowledge is our best interpretation of observed phenomena at any given time. As Barnes observes, Newton was not wrong and Einstein correct; both presented systems of knowledge which proved most useful at that particular stage in the development of their field of knowledge. What this suggests is that scientific knowledge is actually uncertain knowledge, provisional upon a better interpretation of what is known of the physical world. This view is not necessarily derogatory towards the status of scientists or science itself, but it does raise questions about how to approach the presentation of science in displays (Barnes, 1985, pp. 64–71).

The tradition of museums and science centres as institutions of inspiration for an impressionable audience remains strong today. Arguments in support of hands-on science exhibitions are often couched in terms of the recruitment benefits which will result. Young visitors will be so enthralled that they will choose to study science, and some will go to university to provide a pool of future investigators. Whether contemporary science centres achieve these results only time will tell. It will certainly be interesting to know whether those inspired to careers in science through visits to centres such as the Exploratory or Techniquest in the UK or the Exploratorium in the US regard the hands-on displays they found so fascinating as relevant to the study or practice of science. They may do, although one suspects that their explanations will more likely be couched in terms of the theories they have learnt in the course of their education. What science centres do not generally make clear is that the demonstrations they present to the public are part of an existing knowledge system. There is a danger that science is presented as simplistic truth, a mirror image of a 'real' physical world. The nature of scientific knowledge is, however, more complex and, in certain cases, more problematic.

Those involved in science centres may respond to this problem by underlining their concern simply to inspire by stunning visual displays, claiming that too much explanatory material would deaden the impact. That, of course, would depend on the presentation of that explanatory material. It is both arrogant and naive of such institutions to believe that their audience is incapable of understanding their observations and experiences within a particular cognitive framework. After all, the displays are intended to arouse curiosity; they should be designed to provide answers appropriate to the science they present.

Let us return to discussion of the nature of scientific knowledge and the ways in which changes in the knowledge system occur. I have suggested that science at any given time in history involves not just isolated theories, but frameworks of knowledge within which investigations are structured and which provide the basis for explaining experimental data and observations. Major shifts in ideas involve the development of alternative frameworks which provide more powerful explanatory tools for particular observations or problems. Often, however, there is great resistance to the rejection of one set of ideas in favour of another even when the new system can be shown to solve many difficult anomalies. It is natural for people to be more comfortable with what they have been schooled to believe than with what they are invited to consider. Ideas and theories are then seen to play a social as well as cognitive function, providing a common bond between a community of practitioners, a means of uniting a group through adherence to its norms.

If we consider the intimate nature of fact, theory and pre-existing belief together with the social function of scientific knowledge, we begin to build up a view of knowledge as produced not by inspired individuals, but by communities of scientists who in turn belong to broader social structures. Scientists bring to their work not only the experiences of their academic discipline, but their experiences as active members of society. It is impossible for any person to discard the cultural norms in which he or she had been brought up when they enter the laboratory. They bring with them not just the sensory experiences accumulated through childhood and the literary traditions of their education and culture, but also interests which may rest in economic concerns or in technical requirements. Scientific knowledge, according to this view, can never be context-independent, but is embedded in the religious, political, and economic mores of the people who produce it. This is not to suggest that science should be any less highly regarded because of its social nature: rather, I am arguing for the inevitability of that nature (Barnes, 1977).

If science is regarded, therefore, as an aspect of general culture, interpretations of scientific change need to adopt very broad historical perspectives. For example, a vigorous scientific controversy involved the reception of Charles Darwin's ideas about evolution presented in his 1859 book *The Origin of Species* (Mason, 1962, pp. 412–34). Richard Owen (1804–1892), director of the Natural History Museum soon to establish itself in South Kensington, was severely critical of Darwin's views and probably provided the ammunition used by the Bishop of Oxford, Samuel Wilberforce, in his attack on Darwin's theories at the British Association meeting in Oxford in 1860. Darwin's ideas were ably defended by Thomas Henry Huxley, Professor of Geology at the School of Mines. Darwinism, in fact, became widely accepted in this country, although arguments continued to rage about its compatibility with religion in the US for many decades. Why did Darwin's ideas find favour? Within the framework of evolution he suggested there were many theoretical problems, not least the mechanism by which characteristics were inherited. The data upon which he based the theory – the fossil record – could not wholly support his ideas. Darwin explained away the problem as lack of data: the fossil record was incomplete, he claimed, both because naturalists had not collected all available specimens and because not all examples of organisms that had existed through time had been preserved. Despite these major logical problems, Darwinism has proved a powerful paradigm, providing problems for biologists to explore and scope for modification of the theory to explain unexpected observations. One reason which has been put forward to explain the acceptance of evolutionary theory is the congruence between Darwinism and the ethos of liberalism which was prevalent in Britain in the 1850s and 1860s. Liberalism, like Darwinism, stressed the role of the individual, arguing for economic survival of the fittest. Within this economic doctrine, *laissez-faire* policies predominated: nothing must interfere with the natural workings of the system. Another reason for the triumph of Darwinism was the concern of Victorian scientists to establish secular cognitive authority. Darwin's theory did not require an omnipotent creator. The debate in Oxford became a struggle between two professional groups, one defending established territory, the other arguing for a knowledge system based on the norms of their emerging community. Huxley and his colleagues wanted to establish their professional right to determine what knowledge about the physical world should be given precedence.

There are other examples of the clash of science with religious authority, but there are also instances of debate which illustrate the social dimension intrinsic within professional argument. For example, Stephen Jay Gould has described the re-interpretation of the fossils of the Burgess Shale, a site in the Rocky Mountains of Canada which since its discovery ninety years ago has yielded a stunningly rich fossil fauna and flora (Gould, 1991). The debate in this case is not between two contemporary sets of scientists, but between an accepted account and a new interpretation. Gould shows how embedded the first account of the fossils presented by Charles Doolittle Walcott was in the Darwinian tradition of evolution which, in the early decades of the twentieth century, presupposed a progression from the simple to the more complex. His account is particularly interesting for us because he has been able to detail how

Walcott 'saw' fossil specimens by the retouching of photographs which reveal the ideas behind his observations. The new view of the structure of the organisms preserved in the Burgess Shale presents a very different view of the evolution of life, suggesting initial high diversity followed by decimation. What survived to form the basis of our modern fauna was contingent upon this event of decimation.

If we accept the nature of science as but one form of culture within our society, albeit a very potent, authoritative form of culture, then we must consider whether science museums as popularisers of that culture present this aspect of scientific knowledge satisfactorily. More recent displays do explore the human side of scientific discovery so that, in general, ideas are not presented as falling from heaven. There is reluctance, however, to be controversial in exhibitions, particularly when a display is being funded by an organisation involved in the subject matter of the display. And herein lies a dilemma. That organisation may be concerned about the prominence given to their particular scientific views. The most obvious examples of this kind of bias which have occurred in recent years concern the presentation of nuclear power at the Science Museum in London and at the Museum of Science and Industry in Manchester. In the first example, there were suggestions that the sponsor had controlled the presentation of material right down to the level of editing text (Young and Levidow, 1984). In the second, although the sponsor, British Nuclear Fuels Ltd., took no part in the development of the design brief, the presentation of the more controversial aspects of this type of power generation, such as the incidence of childhood leukemia associated with nuclear generating sites, clearly reflected the reluctance of any organisation to upset a well-heeled sponsor (Jones, 1992). If scientific knowledge is presented as objective, authoritative and free from interests, then such exhibitions miss opportunities to stimulate informed public debate. Importantly, these missed opportunities mean that debates between two scientific camps will continue to be seen as arguments between correct and incorrect, instead of clashes of interpretation, each valid within their own terms of theory and social and technical interests.

An archeology of knowledge

Museum collections can provide us with valuable insights into the development of particular knowledge systems which cannot be gleaned from the published papers of scientists or their private manuscript sources. There are limits, of course, to this knowledge, but that is true of any historical source. The problem of the archeology of science can be explored by looking at a collection of apparatus which belonged to one man whose experimental work made major contributions to the development of modern thermodynamics, James Prescott Joule (1818–1889) (Cardwell, 1989).

The Joule collection was acquired by the North West Museum of Science and Technology in 1969. There are a number of electromagnets which, like much of the apparatus Joule used in his experiments, were made by him, together with instruments purchased from well-known makers of the mid nineteenth century (Butler, 1989a).

The electromagnets date from Joule's earliest experimental work undertaken at a comparatively young age. By 1838 when he was still not 20 years old, he had established some form of laboratory or workshop at his father's house. Here he constructed numerous soft iron electromagnets, searching for a design which would produce a magnet capable of useful work. These magnets aroused Joule's curiosity as to the nature of electricity, and he began investigating the strength of current produced by certain batteries. He built his own galvanometers to measure the current, and although they do not survive within the collection, we do have his detailed descriptions of their delicacy and their accuracy. By 1841 he was investigating the heating effects of electric currents using the glass cylinder and jar which form important artefacts within the collection.

Joule extended this interest in temperature changes by looking at the thermal effects produced by a dynamo powered by falling weights. From these experiments he was able to propose a value for the mechanical equipment of heat: 838 foot lbs. equivalent to one degree Fahrenheit in a pound of water. The following year he established a further value for the mechanical equipment of heat by measuring the thermal effects produced when gases are compressed and then allowed to expand. For these experiments, in which he anticipated the temperature changes would be slight, Joule commissioned from John Benjamin Dancer, one of Manchester's best-known nineteenth-century instrument makers, thermometers and a travelling microscope to enable the scale of each thermometer to be calibrated for each experiment. The microscope survives as testimony to Dancer's skill in producing high-quality, attractive instruments (Wetton, 1991).

Perhaps the most important objects in the collection are the two paddlewheels constructed to investigate his idea that heat could be generated by friction. One of the paddlewheels is actually a replica of the apparatus Joule used in the original experiments undertaken in 1846. The other was made by Joule and used in later experiments. The experiments involved turning the paddlewheels in a bath of water by letting falling weights operate a pulley system. He equated the rise in temperature with the friction produced through the force of the falling weight. From his data he calculated a value for the mechanical equivalent of heat. Joule repeated these experiments with slight modifications in 1849 and 1878, establishing ever more accurate values for his equivalence. In all these experiments he used Dancer's thermometers.

Joule's experimental work and his ideas about the conservation of forces in nature provided quantitative evidence for the articulation by William Thomson (later Lord Kelvin) of the first law of thermodynamics. Joule went on to work with Thomson in investigations of the thermal effects of gases in motion.

Although his most significant research was effectively complete by the 1850s, Joule continued to experiment with different measuring devices and to investigate electricity and magnetism throughout his life. Among his instruments is a magnificent Dancer microscope which he probably purchased in the late 1850s. There is also a blowpipe, a chemical balance, and a beautifully crafted, accurate rule which together indicate the range of experiments he undertook.

What can be learnt from the instruments used by this great experimentalist which survive as the Joule collection? First of all, they indicate to us the breadth of Joule's associations. Throughout his career he was an important figure within the Manchester scientific community centred in the 1840s on the Literary and Philosophical Society. William Sturgeon, inventor of the soft iron electromagnet, was clearly an inspiring figure to the young man. Sturgeon had moved to Manchester from London to organise the Victoria Gallery of Science. Dancer's instrument-making skills and his practical advice were also influential in developing Joule's experimental techniques. Together with Lyon Playfair, with whom Joule worked on a long series of experiments on atomic volume, and John Mercer, a manufacturing chemist from Oakenshaw, Lancashire, this group shared a common interest in practical matters, and a concern for inventing. Mercer was responsible for the process of treating cotton with strong alkali to ensure a good uptake of dye. Together with John Benjamin Dancer, he carried out a number of photographic experiments; the Museum of Science and Industry holds a photograph on cloth taken by Mercer of the Manchester instrument-maker. Within Joule's circle of scientific friends, the focus was on the observable, the innovative, the practical; there was little emphasis on metaphysical concepts.

Joule's horizons were, however, not confined to this Manchester community. Some of his instruments were purchased from London makers, R. and G. Knight, Casella and Watkins and Hill, and from instrument-makers in Paris. He clearly suffered few financial constraints to his experimenting and was well informed about the availability of instruments. He also often made his own instruments and apparatus. Manchester's manufacturing industry ensured that supplies of wrought iron tubing, gunmetal and other components were easily available. A supply of wrought iron was crucial to the construction of the electromagnets, which required careful annealing and preparation. For Joule, science involved craft skills. His laboratory was as much an engineering workshop with furnace and lathe, as an area for delicate experimentation. His science was not equivalent to the popular experimenting of the late eighteenth century which involved highly polished instruments of great beauty. Experimenting for him was also generally an individual activity – only the apparatus designed for the investigations of gases in motion required more than one person to manipulate.

The objects associated with Joule's work show that science can only be fully appreciated as a social activity. Manchester's engineering industries provided the physical material for the apparatus which was designed to investigate electricity as a potential source of industrial power. To ignore the context of Manchester as one of Britain's most productive industrial cities would reduce our appreciation of Joule's work. In turn, his apparatus emphasises the importance of context.

There are, of course, clearly limits to what can be learnt from objects. Some deteriorate through time, so our ability to judge their importance or appreciate their original characteristics is reduced. I am doubtful whether any attempts, for example, of reconstructing experiments from Joule's apparatus would serve much purpose. His extraordinary claims for the accuracy of his observations could not be meaningfully tested with apparatus which has inevitably suffered the ravages of time. However, reconstructions of experimental procedures are not necessarily useless to the historian. If done with the realisation that the historian is bringing new, different skills to the experiment, then certain valuable insights may be gained. For example, it is instructive to use an eighteenth-century microscope in order to appreciate the difficulties in both the mechanical design and the aberration produced by the lenses, but it is necessary to bear in mind that modern users are not 'seeing' as eighteenth-century microscopists would see: our opinion of the image will be different to theirs.

There are comparatively few professional historians of science. Objects from science museum collections are not often used for historical investigations, and our understanding of the past is sadly the poorer for this omission. Objects, because they formed part of the day-to-day life of the investigator, can tell us about the nature of that activity. Their appearance can inform us sometimes of the regard in which that occupation must have been held. Again, microscopes provide good examples. In the mid nineteenth century, their shining brass stands symbolised middle-class endeavours to self-improvement through study of the natural world. Often they would be exhibited within the home under glass domes, serving an ornamental as well as a purely instrumental function.

Objects can therefore provide information about how scientists have undertaken their investigations. We can build on the accounts of experimental work by looking at the designs of apparatus to gain an appreciation of the intimate nature of theory and practice in science. By surveying collections of individuals, we can map their association with other investigators and with instrument-makers. Museum collections hold insights into the social nature of science and can help us build up our understanding of the structuring of the knowledge system. It is up to curators to think critically and imaginatively about their collections and to present interpretations which will help visitors appreciate what science is really about.

Directors of science museums seem to have no difficulty in attracting visitors through their doors. Visitors expect to experience spectacular experiments, to see apparatus associated with the most significant scientific discoveries and to marvel at the engineering techniques of modern industrial society. They do not expect and certainly do not want lessons in philosophy. Nevertheless, the potency of scientific achievement in modern society is such that museums must, if they are to fulfil their public duty, examine knowledge and practice critically. The challenge is to embed the critical approach within the design of the exhibition so that the impact of the phenomenon or theory is not lost, but is enhanced by being understood in terms of contemporary culture and economic interests. Scientific apparatus must be 'read' by curators in the same way as works of art or archeological specimens are considered. The objects of science must be interpreted for visitors, their significance shown within particular cognitive frameworks, which are themselves indivisible from the societies in which they were formed.

7. The challenge of the new century

Science museums throughout the world share a common mission of public enlightenment. They have undertaken this task in many different ways. Some concentrate on demonstrating past achievements; others use hands-on exhibits to encourage a sense of exploration among visitors; many combine a range of display techniques to create dramatic effects to impress on visitors the impact of science and technology on daily life.

Museums displaying the technology of industry have multiplied since the 1960s. They were set up not to educate, but to commemorate. These institutions preserve the machinery and sometimes the skills of industries which have not survived the recent technological revolutions. The great open air museums such as Ironbridge, the Black Country Museum at Dudley and Beamish in the North East of England have followed the traditions of the Scandinavian folk museums, changing the meaning of the term 'museum' for both visitors and professionals. Their popularity and success owe much to the interest in heritage which became particularly strong during the 1980s. Although the prime objective of these projects was to preserve the past, many have established vigorous educational programmes. They offer support materials to help teachers use their displays to best educational advantage, and supply worksheets and activities for the children themselves. Their emphasis on the social aspects of industrial society has helped humanise technology by presenting the economic implications of many of the developments which have shaped modern industrial society.

These various types of science museums have all proved popular visitor attractions. More than 3 million people visit the Chicago Museum of Science and Industry each year, for example, and about

1.5 million visitors are expected annually at the London Science Museum. Such success requires considerable effort, not only on the part of curators and designers in creating interesting and appealing displays, but also on the part of directors to ensure adequate funding and appropriate marketing. The late 1980s has proved a difficult economic period for all institutions, and there is considerable pressure on museum directors to maintain high levels of visitors within strict expenditure budgets. For those museums which charge entry, visitor numbers play a vital role within the annual balance sheet. In the rest of this chapter the main challenges which face institutions as we approach the twenty-first century will be explored.

Recent reports indicate that all museums in the UK are currently in a state of transition (Middleton, 1990; Audit Commission, 1991). The most fundamental change concerns the attitude of staff, especially curators, to the nature of their institutions. Until the last decade or so, most curators concerned themselves with their collections, assiduously adding material when opportunities presented themselves, researching where necessary and providing public access by displaying objects. At the heart of the museum was the concept of 'public service'. Museums were there to provide cultural amenities, available to all at no charge. More recently, these ideals have been challenged by the more aggressive market-orientated style of the independent museums established since the 1970s. In these museums curators are more concerned to develop displays which will satisfy an audience which has paid to enter the museum, and less concerned with the development of collections for their own sake.

Museums are changing for other reasons also. Until about twenty years ago, museums and art galleries faced little competition from other providers of culture and leisure. Today, the leisure industry is big business, with individuals and families able and willing to spend money on entertainment. The population trends forecast for the UK during the 1990s indicate that this market looks set to grow, presenting new opportunities for leisure providers, particularly those which cater for children. The number of 5-to-14-year-olds will probably increase by about 1 million and the number of adults between 30 and 44 years of age will also rise by about 1 million (Middleton, 1990, p. 26). These together constitute the family market for which science and technology museums cater so effectively.

Compared to the early decades of the century, the British population is much better educated: an increasing number of young people are leaving school with formal qualifications and, by the turn of the century, the proportion of the population with further and higher education qualifications will have increased significantly. If museums are to continue to satisfy their visitors, this growing sophistication must be acknowledged and taken account of when planning exhibitions and other visitor facilities.

Museums face strong competition as they seek to attract these new family groups over the next decade. Television is no longer a luxury in modern homes but an accepted item of equipment providing information about current affairs, entertainment, and a means of self-education. An increasing number of homes possess videos providing access to film entertainment as well, and high-quality audio equipment is also common place.

For individuals and families looking for leisure facilities outside the home there is much to choose from. The retailing industry has been successful in establishing the concept of 'leisure shopping' first introduced in North America. With the development of major new covered centres such as the Gateshead Metro Centre, and themed shopping areas such as that in Covent Garden in London and the Albert Dock in Liverpool, shopping has become a pleasant pastime. Heritage attractions including the Jorvik Viking Centre in York, Cadbury World in Bourneville, Wigan Pier (perhaps the best known development of recent years) and the White Cliffs Experience at Dover compete for visitors, offering professionally packaged exhibitions often linked to themed retail outlets. The fastest growing sector of the leisure industry is the large theme parks, the best known and most spectacular recent development being EuroDisney near Paris. These developments offer a complete day out and often target their entertainment at children by catering for both teenagers and the very young.

If museums are to remain major competitors to other providers of leisure and culture, they must adapt to these changing market conditions. In his recent report, Victor Middleton argues that to compete effectively museums must play their rivals at their own game: employ the techniques of professional managers, become outward-looking and visitor-orientated and concentrate less on the collections themselves (Middleton, 1990, pp. 51–68). In effect he is suggesting that they must become more like theme parks or heritage centres. Although he is undoubtedly correct in stressing the need for museums to become more administratively efficient, it should be possible to compete, not by following the competition blindly, but by museums developing their own special strengths. Robert Hewison, in his critiques of the heritage industry, has repeatedly pleaded for more emphasis on scholarship within displays (Hewison, 1987, p. 144; Hewison, 1991). He is not arguing for a return to the detailed, esoteric labelling of the Science Museum displays of the 1900s, but for exhibitions which present historical material to visitors by stimulating their imaginations and challenging them with thought-provoking ideas. His arguments apply, of course, equally to displays about contemporary issues as to those focusing on science and technology. It is the collections and the information amassed by curators which make museums special. The challenge of the 1990s is to find ways of communicating that information, taking account of the increasing educational sophistication of the potential audience.

Many museum professionals regard scholarship as under serious threat as a result of the changing role of the curator (Museums and Galleries Commission, 1988, p. 6). Shortage of money, often resulting in reductions in staff numbers, have reduced the time curators can spend on scholarly activities such as preparing academic papers. However, perhaps we need to appraise what is meant by scholarship. When Robert Hewison refers to scholarship, he does not mean the research ideal pursued in universities. He is, I think, arguing for greater depth in all displays; for curators to seek out new material to present to visitors in such a way as to encourage a rethink of a particular subject. Neil Cossons, Director of the Science Museum in London, professes considerable commitment to the ideal that scholarship should be at the heart of the museum (Cossons, 1991). Since becoming Director in 1986, the staffing structure of the museum has been reorganised, with the formation of five divisions following largely functional categories: Collections Management; Research and Information; Public Services; Marketing and Resource Management. By replacing the subject departments with this new structure, Cossons hopes to be able to structure teams to tackle particular projects by drawing on museum-wide talent. He also hopes to release certain curators from collections-based activities to allow them to pursue research, including the preparation of scholarly catalogues. Cossons is well aware of the educational aims of the founders of the museum he now manages, and has appointed as Head of Research and Information a specialist in the public understanding of science. John Durant has been involved in projects to investigate the level of scientific literacy among the general public, and is now in charge of the department which will provide the material the museum could use to improve visitors' understanding of science and its social implications (Thomas and Durant, 1987).

Science Museum displays have always been based on detailed research as befits a great national institution, and the threat to scholarship of the changes of the 1970s is relatively minor compared to the problems facing curators in smaller independent museums or local authority institutions. However, it is encouraging that its Director, with his background in the competitive world of the independent sector, should make such visible and clearly-stated commitments to strengthening the academic depth of the institution. The kind of scholarship that Cossons envisages represents long-term investment in the development of the museum. Smaller, poorer institutions would find this kind of investment difficult to justify during times of financial stringency. What they can and should be able to do is to ensure that the preparation of exhibits involves a high level of scholarship, so that the product offered to visitors stands out as a quality contribution to our understanding of the subject in question.

Such commitments are not always easy for institutions to make. Throughout the 1980s, public spending on museums and galleries in Britain has not kept pace with pay settlements or with inflation. Many curators are expected to be administrators and marketing officers, as well as carers of collections and developers of exhibitions. However, museums are in danger of doing themselves a disservice if they neglect the unique treasures they offer to a public ever-more receptive to the facilities which could be provided.

The financial pressures on museums show signs of increasing rather than lessening during the 1990s. Local authorities are currently forced to keep their spending within very strict limits in order to avoid financial penalties from the Treasury. Discretionary services such as museums are vulnerable and are coming under special scrutiny. Authorities want to be able to demonstrate value for money. Performance indicators are often used to evaluate effi-ciency in the various functions of the museum. Greater emphasis is being placed on good management and careful administration. Such changes, of course, are to be welcomed if they lead to better museums (and not simply better organised pieces of paper).

Treasury grants from the Office of Arts and Libraries to museums such as the Science Museum, the National Museums on Merseyside and the Museum of Science and Industry in Manchester have suffered similar erosion during the 1980s. One way of bridging the deficit, as mentioned above, is to charge admission. Charges to national museums were first introduced in 1974 for about three months. During that period the number of visitors to the British Museum fell by 60 per cent (Wilson, 1989, p. 100). The measure was controversial, challenging a long-held belief in the principle of free access to public institutions of culture. In the 1980s, charges have been reintroduced at several of London's national museums. In all cases the number of visitors fell dramatically after the initial introduction, before recovering again slightly. Comparisons of attendance at English national museums identifying those which charge and those which are free indicate that admission charges have caused visitor figures to decline (Audit Commission, 1991, p. 25). However, whatever one's attitude towards charging, such bald statistics must be considered with care. When museums which do not make a charge for entrance count their visitors, there is every incentive to overestimate the number of people passing an electronic device or a warden with a mechanical counter; the till roll, by contrast, gives not an estimate, but an accurate account of each category of visitor.

In Britain, entry charges to public sector museums remain an emotive issue. David Wilson, director of the British Museum from 1977 until 1991, championed the cause of free access, citing the 20 per cent increase in visitors to the British Museum compared to the 31 per cent fall in visitors to the V. and A. over the three years after the latter's introduction of voluntary charges (Wilson, 1989, p. 101–3). Wilson also points out that the administrative costs of levying charges are not inconsiderable, and admission charges would also mean the loss to the British Museum of voluntary donations and a possible reduction in revenue from catering and commercial outlets in the museum. However, for Wilson, as for his successor Robert Anderson, the overwhelming argument against charging admission is the ideal of free access enshrined in the founding instruments of these great public institutions.

In contrast some directors, including Neil Cossons and Patrick Greene of the Museum of Science and Industry in Manchester, remain convinced that today's visitors expect to pay, that they get more out of their visit because they have parted with cash, and that when properly administered, entry charges can make a vital contribution to any museum's budget, ensuring that museums can be renewed by fresh displays. A recent House of Commons Committee has recommended that all the national museums and galleries consider introducing charges (House of Commons, 1990). Should this happen, the pressure on local authority museums to charge admission will become difficult to withstand.

Charging is a necessity rather than an option for most independent museums. In order to survive they must attract sufficient visitors. The challenge of the 1990s for them is, therefore, to identify new visitors; to make sure that visitors are offered attractive opportunities to spend more money during the course of their visit either on food and drink or on souvenirs; and to raise capital sums from charitable trusts and commercial organisations to fund new facilities which may include measures to improve the care and management of collections.

Some independents approach the raising of capital with gusto. Ironbridge have laid out their shopping list of facilities in a brochure sponsored by British Steel (Rayner, 1989). The brochure outlines the various projects which the museum would like to undertake during the 1990s to provide improved catering and accommodation for visitors and various new projects intended for Ironbridge. The hope is that different projects will appeal to different commercial organisations. The museum is also exploring how partnerships between themselves and companies involved in the development of certain facilities might be beneficial. How much is achieved remains to be seen. However, it is clear that extracting money from any organisation is not easy in the economic recession which, in 1992, shows no signs of abating.

Raising money from commerce is vital to many public institutions, enabling them to fund high-quality exhibitions. The management of sponsorship has become an art in itself, particularly for science and technology museums where sponsors may have been approached because of their associations with the subject of the exhibition. Museums in the UK have tended to avoid the approach taken by the Chicago Museum of Science and Industry where sponsors have, since the 1940s, provided not only cash but also exhibits. Instead, museums in Britain have encouraged a hands-off approach, offering sponsors their own professionalism in presentation. The advantage to the sponsor lies, not so much in the message of the exhibition, but in the association with an institution of culture and education. Exhibitions also give companies which depend upon a relatively highly-educated workforce the chance to encourage young people to continue studying science and to consider science-based careers. In the 1990s these advantages may not be enough to persuade industry of the value to them in parting with hard-pressed public relations budgets.

Those science and technology museums which include working machinery in their displays could face particular problems during the 1990s. Many, such as the Helmshore Textile Museum in Lancashire, have depended since opening on demonstrators previously employed in the industry. These demonstrators operate the machinery, explain the significance of the processes and answer any questions. Visitors have come to appreciate the first-hand knowledge of technology such individuals can pass on. As time goes on, however, the skills and knowledge these men and women possess will leave museums as they reach retirement. The value of their memories is immeasurable and can never be replaced. Their knowledge of operating machines and keeping them in good working order can, however, be captured, and museums must take action to make sure that some kind of apprentice training is available so that skills can be continually renewed.

The restoration and care of industrial heritage presents particular problems of an ethical and practical nature for museums. The craft of conservation of works of art and archeological objects has established clear ethical guidelines distinguishing restoration from conservation. In the former the object will undergo radical treatment to ensure that its appearance is acceptable and is as near as possible to its original form. When undergoing conservation, in contrast, the treatments used will be reversible – will halt the further deterioration of the object, but will not significantly alter the form of the object. The dilemmas facing those caring for industrial artefacts are exactly the same. Should machines be conserved in the form in which they have been found, or should they be restored so that they can function again in the way they were designed? The questions are usually not clear-cut and often involve considerations of cost and whether the object is intended for display or simply as a historical record. Perhaps the most important part of the process is the decisions about what kind of techniques are appropriate to apply to a particular object. These decisions must be made through consultation between the technician or engineer who is to carry out the work and the curator, whose responsibility it is to care for and preserve the object. Both individuals must together make sure that whatever is done to the object is properly recorded. As in other branches of conservation, the greatest need is to provide the means of training in techniques. The Science Museum in London has over the past few years organised short courses, intended as part of broader schemes of training for technicians involved in industrial conservation. Through this formal instruction and the training provided on-the-job, the skills and knowledge necessary to keep the wheels of industrial heritage turning should be maintained.

The machinery discarded by industry during the 1970s and 1980s has given way to equipment which is generally less immediately attractive than its predecessors. In research laboratories, modern instruments are sometimes enormous pieces of equipment housed in faceless boxes. Both generations of objects present curators with almost impossible collecting decisions. Quality storage space, necessary to ensure that equipment with delicate electronic mechanisms do not deteriorate, is very expensive. Curators are therefore under pressure to collect only those items which will represent in the future the most significant of current equipment. This is an immensely difficult task because modern technology can change so rapidly that historical perspective is impossible before objects have disappeared. The National Museums of Scotland have tackled the problem by using the knowledge of an experienced practitioner, a chemist, Dr Bob Nuttall who, on secondment from his academic post, surveyed the availability of modern scientific equipment in laboratories in Scotland and made recommendations about which available items should be collected. No-one can guarantee such decisions will be infallible, but it is certainly a more constructive approach than to do nothing or to collect merely passively – an approach which can lead to very unbalanced collections.

Once collected, decisions must be made as to whether the various pieces of equipment are to be maintained in working order or simply allowed to rest as a static archive. Either way, the importance of maintenance documentation is paramount. Manuals provide enormously valuable information, occasionally documenting the individual history of the machine. Manuals, however, are often not sufficient to provide the means for maintaining modern scientific equipment in working order. Only manufacturers have the essential expertise. If they can be persuaded to adopt certain key machines and provide the necessary technical assistance, then it is possible to preserve such technology in dynamic form. Close relationships, such as those established between the Deutsches Museum and Germany's scientific and technical industries, can ensure that such expertise is available when required.

How will designers and curators face the problems of displaying modern scientific and technological equipment? Faced with the difficulties of interpreting instruments whose functions are probably impossible for the majority of museum visitors to comprehend, will museums be tempted to concentrate more on principles and concepts and to use hands-on exhibits? Will the obsession with nostalgia continue to demand yet more period sets?

The replies to these questions are impossible to give with complete certainty. However, it seems more than likely that, in the UK at least, science centres such as Techniquest in Cardiff and the Exploratory in Bristol will remain committed to object-free, hands-on displays. Both are essentially independent institutions, very much reliant on visitor receipts and grants to finance their operation. Collecting objects would be a costly and onerous activity for them to embark upon and one which presents little advantage.

For those museums with collections, the question of whether to pursue hands-on displays is perhaps the more intriguing. Galleries such as Xperiment! in Manchester and Launch Pad in London have consciously excluded objects and conventional display techniques such as graphic panels. One result has been to present scientific concepts rather baldly, allowing visitors opportunities to explore phenomena, but in many instances not providing the means of discovering how the principle or phenomenon is exploited in technology or what its significance is within a wider knowledge system. This absence of context has invited many criticisms. Perhaps those criticisms will be met by a new genre of hands-on displays such as Scientrific at Catalyst in Widnes, where interactive exhibits have been complemented by displays of historic objects and computer databases providing background information.

The fascination of the general public with the past shows no signs of abating. Exhibitions documenting past achievements using authentic material will probably always attract wide audiences.

Perhaps the biggest challenge for museums dedicated to public education is to find ways of exploring the less comfortable aspects of science and technology. Today, the scientific profession comprises a hierarchy of people and institutions competing for funds in a race for knowledge. Awareness of issues such as recognition for the discovery of particular theories and the problems of obtaining financial support for research would broaden the public's understanding of science and technology.

We noted in Chapter 1 that military support for science and technology has become increasingly important since the Second World War. Many scientists find the association with the technology of war uncomfortable. However, the relationship exists. The military have gained enormous strategic advantages from technological innovations; research carried out for military purposes has often proved of fundamental importance to the development of particular branches of science and technology. Science museums should not ignore this relationship, particularly as political events in the Eastern Bloc since 1990 have eased tension and removed the threat of global military conflict between the two super-powers. This might be good news for the citizens of the world, but will it mean less money for science?

The museum visitor of the 1990s expects multi-media displays. The competitors in the leisure industry are often skilled communicators. Granada Studios Tours has all the techniques of the television industry at its disposal; Disneyland can rely on sixty years' experience of conjuring make-believe. The most successful museum displays combine professional video and audio-visual presentations with the immediacy of original artefacts to create an experience for the visitor which is unique and cannot be matched elsewhere. Visitors go away entertained but also educated, albeit informally.

Within the British education system, one of the most significant changes in recent years has been the introduction of the national curriculum, which has established science as part of the core curriculum for children joining school at 5 years of age until the school leaving age of 16. The introduction of science teaching at primary level has presented an enormous challenge to many schools. For museums this has brought an audience of primary school teachers hungry for assistance. These teachers want to bring their classes to learn from displays. They also want curators and museum educationalists to advise them on how to do experiments and problem-solving activities in class. Primary schools often base their teaching on topics which can provide material for different subjects within the curriculum. Museums can provide ideal material for such teaching methods. Many science centres have worked with organisations such as the British Association for the Advancement of Science, whose schemes for Young Investigators have brought informal science teaching into many schools. Other initiatives, such as problem-solving competitions and science drama activities can also serve to complement the new formal courses taught at primary and secondary level. There can be no doubt that the educational reforms of the late 1980s have created a substantial new market for the services of science museums. It is for museums themselves to take advantage of the opportunities and to attract through their doors a new generation of museum visitors.

The broadening of science teaching within the school system should bring long-term benefits to museums. Future generations should be more scientifically literate than their parents. They should become aware of the importance of science and technology to the economic and political future of the subject, and more concerned to keep themselves well informed. Science museums should be prepared to become public educators, presenting not just scientific concepts, but also the issues surrounding the development of technology, however uncomfortable or difficult those subjects might be.

Science museums in Britain, North America and many countries of Europe came into being as agents of public education. Their founders hoped they would spread the gospel of technology, showing visitors scientific achievements. Many have become such important archives of the past that their educational role has become somewhat obscured. However, such is the general ignorance among the adult population in Britain, at least, of basic science and its social implications, that in our ever-more technologically dependent society the need for public educators is as crucial as ever. Science museums, by providing education through entertainment, can fulfil the original aims of their founders, acting both as advocate and teacher.

Appendix: Useful addresses

This is not an exhaustive list of science museums but provides a brief catalogue of most of the major types of institutions presenting exhibitions relating to science, technology and industry.

Beamish, The North of England Open Air Museum, Beamish, County Durham, DH9 0RG.

Black Country Museum, Tipton Road, Dudley, West Midlands, DY1 4SQ.

Birmingham Museum of Science and Technology, Newhall Street, Birmingham, West Midlands, B3 1RZ.

Boston Children Museum, Museum Wharf, 300 Congress Street, Boston, Massachusetts 02210, USA.

The Brooklyn Children's Museum, 145 Brooklyn Avenue, Brooklyn, New York 11213, USA.

Buxton Micrarium, The Crescent, Buxton, Derbyshire, SK17 6BQ.

California Museum of Science and Industry, 700 State Drive, Los Angeles, California 90037, USA.

Capital Children's Museum, 800 Third Street NE, Washington, DC 20002, USA.

Catalyst, Museum of the Chemical Industry, Gossage Building, Mersey Road, Widnes, Cheshire, WA8 0DF.

Cité des Sciences and de l'Industrie, La Villette, 30 avenue Corentin Cariou, 75019 Paris, France.

The Computer Museum Museum Wharf, 300 Congress Street, Boston, MA 02210, USA.

Dallas Health and Science Museum, Box 26407, Fair Park, Dallas, Texas 75226, USA.

Deutsches Museum, D-800 Munich 26, West Germany.

ECSITE, European Collaborative for Science, Industry and Technology Exhibitions, c/o Heureka, The Finnish Science

Centre, Tiedepuisto 1, PO Box 166, SF-01301 Vantaa, Finland.

Exploratorium, 3601 Lyon Street, San Francisco, California 94123, USA.

The Exploratory, Bristol Old Station, Temple Meads, Bristol, BS1 6QU.

Franklin Institute Science Museum, 20th Street and Benjamin Franklin Parkway, Philadelphia, Pennsylvania 19103, USA.

Green's Mill, Belvoir Hill, Sneinton, Nottingham, NG2 4QB.

Hampshire Technology Centre, Romsey Road, Winchester, Hampshire SO22 5PJ.

Helmshore Textile Museum, Holcombe Road, Helmshore, Rossendale, Lancashire, BB4 4NP.

Heureka, The Finnish Science Centre, Tiedepuisto 1, PO Box 166, SF-01301 Vantaa, Finland.

Ironbridge Gorge Museum, Ironbridge, Telford, Shropshire, TF8 7AW.

Lawrence Hall of Science, University of Science, University of California, Centennial Drive, Berkeley, California 94720, USA.

Macclesfield Silk Museum, Heritage Centre, Roe Street, Macclesfield, SK11 6UT.

Maryland Science Center, 601 Light Street, Baltimore, Maryland 21230, USA.

The Museum of American History, The Smithsonian, Washington, DC 20560, USA.

Museum of Applied Arts and Sciences incorporating The Powerhouse Museum, The Mint, and Sydney Observatory, 500 Harris Street, Ultimo, Sydney, New South Wales, Australia.

Museum of the History of Science, Old Ashmolean Building, Broad Street, Oxford, OX1 3AZ.

Museum of Science, Science Park, Boston, Massachusetts 02114, USA.

Museum of Science and Industry, 57th Street and Lake Shore Drive, Chicago, Illinois 60637, USA.

Museum of Science and Industry, Liverpool Road Station, Liverpool Road, Castlefield, Manchester, M3 4JP.

Nagoya Municipal Science Museum, 17–22 Sakae 2-Chome, Naka-Ku, Nagoya 460, Japan.

National Museums and Galleries on Merseyside, William Brown Street, Liverpool, L69 3LA.

National Museum of Science and Technology, Lahore-31, Pakistan.

The National Museum of Photography, Film and Television, Prince's View, Bradford, W. Yorkshire, VD1 1NQ.

National Museum of Science and Technology, 1867 St Laurent Boulevard, Ottawa, Ontario K1A OM8, Canada.

National Museums of Scotland, Chambers Street, Edinburgh, EH1 1JF.

The National Railway Museum (part of the Science Museum), Leeman Road, York, YO2 4XJ.

New York Hall of Science, PO Box 1032, Flushing Meadows–Corona Park, Flushing, New York 11352, USA.

Ontario Science Centre, 770 Don Mills Road, Ontario M3C 1T3, Canada.

Oregon Museum of Science and Industry, 4015 Southwest Canyon Road, Portland, Oregon 97221, USA.

Pacific Science Centre, 200 Second Avenue, North, Seattle, Washington 98109, USA.

Pilkington Glass Museum, Prescot Road, St Helens, Merseyside, WA10 3TT.

Rüsselheim Museum, D-6090 Rüsselsheim, Darmstadter Str. 27, Germany.

Questacon, The National Science and Technology Centre, Queen Victoria Terrace, Canberra, ACT 2600, Australia.

Quarry Bank Mill, Styal, Cheshire, SK9 2LA.

Science Museum, Exhibition Road, South Kensington, London, SW7 2DD.

Singapore Science Centre, Science Centre Road, Singapore 22, Republic of Singapore.

Techniquest, 72 Bute Street, Pier Head, Cardiff, CF1 6AA.

Whipple Museum of the History of Science, Free School Lane, Cambridge CB2 3RH.

Wigan Pier, Wigan Pier, Lancashire, WN3 4EU.

Bibliography

Allan, R., 1991, *Beamish: The north of England open air museum. The making of a museum*, Beamish

Anderson, R., 1986, A new start for the nationals, *Museums Journal*, 86(1): 3–6

Anderson, R., 1989, Museums in the making, in J. Calder (ed.), *The wealth of a nation in the National Museums of Scotland*, National Museums of Scotland, Edinburgh, pp. 1–17.

Association of Science and Technology Centres, 1980, *Exploring science: A guide to contemporary science and technology museums*, Association of Science and Technology Centers, Washington

Atrick, R. D., 1978, *The shows of London*, Harvard University Press, Cambridge (Mass.)

Audit Commission, 1991, *The road to Wigan Pier*, HMSO, London

Barnes, B. (ed.), 1972, *Sociology of science*, Penguin, London

Barnes, B., 1977, *Interests and the growth of knowledge*, Routledge, London

Barnes, B., 1985, *About science*, Basil Blackwell, Oxford

BBC North West, 'Heritage: A thing of the past', Close-Up North, programme broadcast 21 November 1991

Bedini, S. A., 1965, The evolution of science museums, *Technology and Culture*, 6: 1–29

Beaver, P., 1970, *The Crystal Palace*, Hugh Evelyn, London

Bellot, H. H., 1929, *University College London, 1826–1926*, London University Press, London

Beetlestone, J., 1987, Techniquest, in S. Pizzey (ed.), *Interactive science and technology centres*, Science Projects Publishing, London, pp. 151–60

Bennett, J. A., 1983, *Science at the Great Exhibition*, Whipple Museum, Cambridge

Bell, A. S. (ed.), 1983, *The Scottish antiquarian tradition: Essays to mark the bicentenary of the Society of Antiquaries of Scotland and its museum 1780–1980*, John Donald, Edinburgh

Bloom, J. N., Powell, E. A., Hicks, E. C., and Munley, M. E., 1984, *Museums for a new century*, American Association of Museums, Washington DC

Brears, P., 1984, Temples of the Muses: the Yorkshire philosophical museums, *Museums Journal, 84* (1): 3–19

Brown, N., 1991, Review of the Information Age, National Museum of American History, Smithsonian Institution, Washington and the Computer Museum, Boston, *Science and Industry Curators Group Newsletter, 9:* 14–16

Brown, O., Butler, S., and Nutall, R. H., 1986, *The social history of the microscope*, Whipple Museum, Cambridge

Bruman, R., 1987, *Cookbook I: A construction manual for Exploratorium exhibits*, 3rd edition, The Exploratorium, San Francisco

Bryden, D. J., 1978, *Selected exhibits in the Whipple Museum of the History of Science*, Whipple Museum, Cambridge

Bunnell, G., 1980, The interplay of old and new, *Museum News, 59:* 5–18

Burrett, F. G., 1982, *Rayner scrutiny of the departmental museums: Science Museum and the Victoria and Albert Museum*, Office of Arts and Libraries, London

Butler, S. V. F., 1981, Science and the education of doctors in the nineteenth century, unpublished Ph.D., UMIST

Butler, S. V. F., 1985, *Atoms, energy and industry: Two centuries of Manchester science*, Greater Manchester Museum of Science and Industry, Manchester

Butler, S. V. F., 1986, A transformation in training: The formation of university medical faculties in Manchester, Leeds, and Liverpool 1870–1884, *Medical History, 30:* 115–32

Butler, S. V. F., 1989a, The universal agent of power, James Prescott Joule, electricity and the equivalent of heat, in J. T. Stock, and M. V. Orna, *Electrochemistry, past and present*, American Chemical Society, Washington DC., pp. 50–62

Butler, S. V. F., 1989b, Local sources and museums, in M. Shortland and A. Warwick (eds.), *Teaching the history of science*, Basil Blackwell, Oxford, pp. 217–26.

Calder, J., 1984, Royal Scottish Museum: The early years, typescript, Department of Education and Public Relations, Royal Scottish Museum, Edinburgh

Calder, J., 1989, *The wealth of a nation in the National Museums of Scotland*, National Museums of Scotland, Edinburgh

Cambridge Philosophical Society, 1936, *Catalogue of a loan exhibition of historic scientific apparatus in Cambridge*, Cambridge Philosophical Society, Cambridge

Cambridge University, 1944, Whipple benefaction, *Cambridge University Reporter*, 24 October: 158

Cambridge University, 1956, Whipple benefaction, *Cambridge University Reporter*, 25 January: 707

Cardwell, D. S. L., 1972, *The organisation of science in England*, Heinemann, London

Cardwell, D. S. L., 1989, *James Joule: A biography*, Manchester University Press, Manchester

Cité des Sciences et de l'Industrie, 1986, Press Kit, Cité des Sciences et de l'Industrie, Paris

Cole, H., 1884, *Fifty years of public work*, Bell, London

The Computer Museum, 1985, *Report, Winter 1984/5, volume II*, The Computer Museum, Boston

Cossons, N., 1982, A new professionalism, *Supplement to Museums Journal, 82*, (3): 1–2

Cossons, N., 1991, Scholarship or self-indulgence?, *Royal Society of Arts Journal, 139*: 184–91

Danilov, V., 1982, *Science and technology centres*, Massachusetts Institute of Technology Press, Cambridge

Danilov, V., 1990, *America's Science Museums*, Greenwood Press, London

Deutsches Museum, 1988, *Guide through the collections*, Deutsches Museum, Munich

English Tourist Board, 1989, *Retail, leisure and tourism*, London

The Exploratorium, 1982, *A Synopsis*, The Exploratorium, San Francisco

Feist, A. and Hutchison, R., 1989, *Cultural Trends, 4*, Policy Studies Institute, London

Fenomena, n.d. (1985), *A short guide through the exhibition*, Fenomena, Rotterdam

Follet, D., 1978, *The rise of the Science Museum under Henry Lyons*, Science Museum, London

Glancy, M. (ed.), 1990, *Hands on! Exploratory exhibit list*, The Exploratory, Bristol

Gombrich, E. H., 1962, *Art and illusion: A study in the psychology of pictorial representation*, Phaidon, London

Gore, M., 1987, Questacon, in S. Pizzey (ed.), *Interactive science and technology centres*, Science Projects Publishing, London, pp. 117–26

Gould, S. J., 1991, *Wonderful life: The Burgess Shale and the nature of history*, Penguin, London

Greenaway, F., 1951, *A short history of the Science Museum*, HMSO, London

Greene, M., 1989, Powering ahead, *Museums Journal, 89* (10): 23–6

Gregory, R. L., 1987, Origins of the Bristol Exploratory, in S. Pizzey (ed.), *Interactive science and technology centres*, Science Projects Publishing, London, pp. 129–49

Gregory, R. L. and Gombrich, E. H., 1973, *Illusion in Art and Nature*, Duckworth, London

Gunther, R. T., 1985, The Story of the Old Asmolean, in A. V. Simcock (ed.), *Robert T. Gunther and the Old Ashmolean*, Museum of the History of Science, Oxford, pp. 1–42

Harris, D., Lawson, J., and Price, J., n.d., *Beamish: The north of England open air museum: A brief guide*, Beamish

Hartley, F. St., 1938, *The Children's Gallery*, HMSO, London

Hein, H., 1990, *The Exploratorium: The museum as laboratory*, Smithsonian Institution Press, Washington

Hewison, R., 1987, *The heritage industry*, Methuen, London

Hewison, R., 1991, The heritage industry revisited, *Museums Journal, 91*(4): 23–6

Hipschman, R., 1980, *Cookbook II: A construction manual for Exploratorium exhibits*, The Exploratorium, San Francisco

Hipschman, R., 1987, *Cookbook III: A construction manual for Exploratorium exhibits*, The Exploratorium, San Francisco

Horne, D., 1984, *The great museum: The re-presentation of history*, Pluto Press, London

House of Commons, Education and Arts Committee, 1990, *Should museums charge: Some case studies*, HMSO, London

Hudson, K., 1987, *Museums of influence*, Cambridge University Press, Cambridge

Hudson, K., 1975, *A social history of museums: What the visitors thought*, Macmillan Press, London

Hudson, K., 1990, *1992: Prayer or promise? The opportunities for Britain's museums and the people who work in them*, Museums and Galleries Commission, HMSO, London

Hunter, M., 1985, The cabinet institutionalised: The Royal Society's Repository and its background, in O. Impey and

A. MacGregor, *The origins of museums: The cabinets of curiosities in sixteenth and seventeenth century Europe*, Clarendon Press, Oxford, pp. 158–68

Ironbridge Gorge Museum, 1986, *Teachers' Handbook*, Ironbridge Gorge Museum

Ironbridge Gorge Museum, 1989, Visitor profile, prepared for Mercury Communications, Ironbridge

Ironbridge Gorge Museum, 1991, Chronology, typescript, Ironbridge Gorge Museum

Ironbridge Gorge Museum, 1991, Visitor statistics, typescript, Ironbridge Gorge Museum

Jones, T., 1985, Through a glass clearly, *New Scientist*, 28 March: 38–9

Jones, T., 1985, Putting a city on display, *New Scientist*, 19/26 December: 40–42

Jones, T., 1992, It's a visible gas: National gas gallery and Energy for the future, *New Scientist*, 4 January: 35–6

Kargon, R. H., 1977, *Science in Victorian Manchester: Enterprise and expertise*, Manchester University Press, Manchester

Kelly, T., 1962, *A history of adult education in Great Britain*, Liverpool University Press, Liverpool

Kennedy, J., 1987, Liverpool Road: a case study, in Manchester Literary and Philosophical Society, *Conservation: The way forward*, Manchester Literary and Philosophical Society, Manchester, pp. 43–50

Kuhn, T. S., 1962, *The structure of scientific revolutions*, University of Chicago Press, Chicago

Lee, E. and Shore, J., 1990, *Mind and body*, Powerhouse Museum, Sydney

Lewis, G., 1984, Introduction, Collections, collectors and museums: a brief world survey; Collections, collectors and museums in Britain to 1920, in J. Thompson (ed.), *Manual of curatorship*, Butterworth, London, pp. 5–53

Lewis, P., 1991, Making or mocking, *Museums Journal, 91*(7): 33–5

Losee, J., 1980, *A Historical introduction to the philosophy of science*, Oxford University Press, Oxford

Lowenthal, D., 1985, *The past is a foreign country*, Cambridge University Press, Cambridge

MacGregor, A., 1985, The cabinet of curiosities in seventeenth century Britain, in O. Impey and A. MacGregor, *The origins of museums: The cabinets of curiosities in sixteenth and seventeenth century Europe*, Clarendon Press, Oxford, pp. 147–58

Magee, B., 1975, *Popper*, Fontana, Glasgow

Markham, S. F., 1938, *The museum and art galleries of the British Isles*, Carnegie UK Trust, Edinburgh

Marriott, N. (ed.), n.d., *The Exploratory's Adventures in Science*, The Exploratory, Bristol

Mason, S. F., 1962, *A history of the sciences*, Collier, New York

Middleton, V., 1990, *New visions for independent museums in the UK*, Association of Independent Museums, Chichester

Miers, H. A., 1928, *A report on the public museums of the British Isles (other than the national museums)*, Carnegie UK Trust, Edinburgh

Montagu, K., 1984, *Boston Children's Museum*, Children's Museum, Boston

Morrell, J. B., 1972, Science and Scottish university reform, *British Journal for the History of Science*, 6: 39–56

Morrell, J. B., 1974, Science in Manchester and the University of Edinburgh, in D. S. L. Cardwell (ed.), *From artisan to graduate*, Manchester University Press, Manchester, pp. 39–54

Moriyama, R., Gretton, R., Omand, D., Miake, T., Yolles, M., 1969, The Centennial Centre of Science and Technology, Toronto, *Canadian Architect*, 39–52

Mueller, G., 1987, Phaenomena, in S. Pizzey (ed.), *Interactive science and technology centres*, Science Projects Publishing, London, pp. 163–78

Museum of Science and Industry, 1983, *Palace of discovery: A photographic reminiscence*, Museum of Science and Industry, Chicago

Museum of Science and Industry, 1984, *1984 Facts Book*, Museum of Science and Industry, Chicago

Museum of Science and Industry, 1984, *Towards the 21st century: 1983 annual report*, Museum of Science and Industry, Chicago

Museum of Science and Industry, 1990, *The uncommon classroom: Annual report 1989*, Museum of Science and Industry, Chicago

Museum of Science and Industry, 1991, *Corporate plan 1991–1996*, Museum of Science and Industry, Manchester

Museum and Galleries Commission, 1988, *The national museums and galleries of the UK*, HMSO, London

Museums Association, 1931, Science Museum's Children's Gallery, *Museums Journal, 31*: 39

Myerscough, J., 1988, *The economic importance of the arts in Britain*, Policy Studies Institute, London

National Institute for the Conservation of Cultural Property, 1984, *Historic buildings: A study on the magnitude of architectural conservation needs in America*, Washington DC

National Science and Technology Centre, 1989, *Report of Activities 1988–1989*, Questacon, Canberra

O'Brien, J. and Donaldson, J., 1989, *The Powerhouse Museum*, Museum of Applied Arts and Sciences, Sydney

Ontario Science Centre, n.d. (1979), *The first ten years*, Ontario Science Centre, Toronto

Ontario Science Centre, 1989, *A window to the world: Annual report*, Ontario Science Centre, Toronto

Oppenheimer, F., 1968, A rationale for a science museum, reprinted from *Curator, 11* (November): 206

Oppenheimer, F., 1980, Exhibit conception and design, typescript of paper presented in Monterey, Mexico, The Exploratorium, San Francisco

Phillips, D., 1989, *Exploring museums: North west England and the Isle of Man*, HMSO, London

Physick, J., 1982, *The Victoria and Albert Museum: The history of its building*, Victoria and Albert Museum, London

Pizzey, S. (ed.), 1987, *Interactive science and technology centres*, Science Projects Publishing, London

Popper, K., 1972a, *The logic of scientific discovery*, third edition, Hutchinson, London

Popper, K., 1972b, *Conjectures and refutations: The growth of scientific knowledge*, 4th edition, Routledge and Kegan Paul, London

Preuss, P., 1982, Please touch, *American Educator*, 6: 18–27

Prince, D., and McLoughlin, B. H., 1987, *Museums UK: The findings of the museums database project*, Museums Association, London

Rayner, L., 1989, *Ironbridge: A pattern for the future*, Ironbridge Gorge Museum, Ironbridge

Reid, T. W., 1899, *Memoirs and Correspondence of Lyon Playfair*, Cassell, London

Report of the Departmental Committee on the Science Museum and the Geological Museum, Part 1, 1911, *Part 2*, 1912–13, HMSO, London

Richards, C. R., 1925, *The industrial museum*, Macmillan, New York

van Riemsdijk, J. and Sharp, P., 1968, *In the Science Museum*, HMSO, London

Rogers, M., 1981, *The measurement of heat and temperature: A history of rich discourse*, The Exploratorium, San Francisco

Rosse, Earl of, 1963, *Survey of provincial museums and galleries*, HMSO, London

Royal Commission on Scientific Instruction and the Advancement of Science, 1872–5, *Report*, 4 volumes, HMSO, London

Royal Commissioners of the Exhibition of 1851, 1852, *Second Report*, HMSO, London

Schouten, J. F., 1966, *The Evoluon: A permanent Philips exhibition*, The Evoluon, Eindhoven

Science Museum, 1876, *Catalogue of special loan collection of scientific apparatus*, HMSO, London

Science Museum, 1938, *Outline guide to exhibits*, HMSO, London

Science Museum, 1957, *The first hundred years*, HMSO, London

Science Museum Review, 1987, HMSO, London

Science Museum, 1991, *Museum collecting policies in modern science and technology*, Science Museum, London

Sekers, D., 1984, Quarry Bank Mill: Growth of a museum on a shoestring, *Museums Journal*, *84*(2): 72–7

Select Committee Report on Department of Science and Art Museums at South Kensington, 1897, HMSO, London

Sharing science: Issues in the development of interactive science and technology, 1989, Nuffield Foundation/COPUS, London

Schirmbeck, P., 1981, The museum of the city of Rüsselsheim, *Museum*, *33*(1): 35–50

Sim, H., 1991, *Experimentations*, Powerhouse Museum, Sydney

Simcock, A. V., 1984, *The Ashmolean Museum and Oxford science 1683–1983*, Museum of the History of Science, Oxford

Simcock, A. V., 1985, *Robert T. Gunter and the Old Ashmolean*, Museum of the History of Science, Oxford

Simcock, A. V., 1987, An ark for the history of science, *Iatul Quarterly*, *1*, 196–215

Smart, J. E., 1976, Museums in Great Britain with scientific and technological collections, Science Museum Paper, London

Smith, S., 1989, The next thirty years, in A. Raistrick, *Dynasty of Ironfounders*, Sessions Book Trust, York, pp. 273–91

Smithsonian Institution, 1927, *Conference on the future of the Smithsonian Institution*, Smithsonian Institution, Washington DC

Smithsonian Institution, 1983, *An overview*, Smithsonian Institution Press, Washington DC

Starr, K., 1982, Exploration and culture: Oppenheimer receives distinguished service award, *Museum News*, November/December: 36–45

Storer, D. J., 1989, *The conservation of industrial collections: A survey*, Science Museum, London

Sudbury, P., 1987, Technology testbed in S. Pizzey (ed.), *Interactive science and technology centres*, Science Projects Publishing, London, pp. 45–52

Sudjic, D., 1990, Science Museum offers Food for Thought, *Sunday Correspondent*, 7 January: 30

Tait, S., 1989, *Palaces of discovery: The changing world of Britain's museums*, Quiller Press, London

Thackray, A., 1974, Natural knowledge in its cultural context: The Manchester model, *American Sociological Review*, 79: 672–709

Thomas, G., 1987, The Inventorium, in S. Pizzey (ed.), *Interactive science and technology centres*, Science Projects Publishing, London, pp. 77–89

Thomas, G. P. and Durant, J. R., 1987, Why should we promote the public understanding of science, *Scientific Literacy Papers*, 1–4

True, W. P., 1946, *The first hundred years of the Smithsonian Institution 1846–1946*, Smithsonian Institution, Washington

Turvey, P., 1991, Recalculating history (Charles Babbage's Difference Engine no. 2), *Museums Journal*, 91 (2): 34–5

University of Cambridge, History of Science Lectures Committee, 1944, *An exhibition of historic scientific instruments and books*, Cambridge

University of Cambridge, History of Science Lectures Committee, 1949, *A guide to the historic scientific instruments in the Whipple Museum of the history of science*, Cambridge

Wetton, J., 1991, John Benjamin Dancer: Manchester instrument maker, *Bulletin of the Scientific Instrument Society*, 29 (June): 4–8

Walker, P. M. B. (ed.), 1988, *Chambers science and technology dictionary*, Chambers and Cambridge University Press, Edinburgh and Cambridge

Wilson, A., 1987, Launch Pad, in S. Pizzey (ed.), *Interactive science and technology centres*, Science Projects Publishing, London, pp. 23–43

Wilson, A., Watt, S., and Quin, M., 1988, *Launch Pad: Science Museum*, Hobsons, Cambridge

Wilson, D., 1989, *British Museum: Purpose and politics*, British Museum Publications, London

Wright, C. W., 1973, *Provincial museums and galleries*, HMSO, London

Young, B. and Levidow, L., 1984, Exhibiting nuclear power: The Science Museum cover-up, *Radical Science, 14*: 53–78

Index